Art of Pursuit

Pursuing something bigger than You

CONTENTS

Acknowledgments vi

Introduction: Art of Pursuit 1

Chapter 1: Identified 4

Chapter 2: Why Me? 13

Chapter 3: The Vision 25

Chapter 4: Product of Focus & Discipline 43

Chapter 5: The Great Opposition 55

Chapter 6: Hidden Potential 64

Chapter 7: The Misfit 73

Chapter 8: Worth It 84

Chapter 9: Masterpiece Donation 97

About The Author 109

DEDICATION

This book truly would've never existed if it had not been for the biggest blessing in my life, teaching me all that I know, always being there for me every step of the way, and most importantly giving me life. You both mean the world to me and I constantly thank God each and every day for blessing me with more than I deserve. Thank you for all that you have done and for being the best role models in my life. You both are the reason I am the woman I am today because of your faithfulness to God, and because of that I forever admire you both in all that you do. I love you mom and dad, more than words will ever describe.

This book is dedicated, with deep love and appreciation to Corey and Tynika Moore.

Love, Lissa.
(P.s daddy's girl, Lizzy)

ACKNOWLEDGMENTS

A wise man named Myles Munroe once said, "When you believe in your dream and your vision, only then it begins to attract its own resources. No one was born to be a failure." This has always been one of my favorite quotes because, over time, I began to see this very thing happen right before my eyes. In fact, this very book is a product of a vision and dream I believed in for so long and little did I know, it would all be possible through great resources and such as a great friend. I would like to give a great thanks to Kyle Dendy in helping me make my vision for this book come to life. If it had not been for your book the *Purpose Playbook*, I wouldn't be doing some of the things I am doing today, and this book would have never actually existed. So, I thank you for your faithfulness to God and the calling He has placed on your life in helping others around the world understand their purpose in life. I've watched God do some incredible things for you and through you, and because of that, you have and always will be a great inspiration to me and all the people you constantly touch around the world. May God continue to bless you in all that you do, as you continue to change the world. #PurposeGang

INTRODUCTION
ART OF PURSUIT

The pursuit in our life is essentially something that gives us a reason to be living. It is the idea of pursuing something we want out of this life, although we often find ourselves pursuing the wrong things, pursuing nothing or settle for things in our own reach. Sometimes, we don't even think for a second in pursuing something that seems beyond our reach or bigger than ourselves. What if I told you, however, that all could change when you fully understand that you can pursue something bigger than you? There are so many great things to pursue in this life, but what happens when in the end, the things you wish to pursue in your life only lead to temporary satisfaction? We pursue all different types of things in our life that drain us, stress us out, and eventually lead to nothing but temporary success and satisfaction that slowly starts to fade away. We all want something worth pursuing that will benefit us for the better and give us the outcomes we wish to see, that last and become something we are able to build upon.

At a young age, I decided I was going to pursue something bigger than myself, but I had no idea it was going to end up changing my life forever. Although being young, I didn't necessarily know what to expect or what I was getting myself into; I was simply just a kid who had big dreams and wanted to see them happen right before my eyes. There were so many things I faced over and over in my life while doing everything in my power to pursue something beyond me. It was a constant thought within me that made me believe that certain things could be done with the right help and guidance. I was grateful and blessed to have great guidance along the way that helped me greatly in the process, but there was also so much I had to learn for myself and things I am still learning as of today. As I got older, I personally went through a process of understanding and learning along the way, methods that helped me in so many ways that I truly believe will do the same for you. In fact, one of the things I've constantly been learning that has helped me tremendously is just how significant the process of the pursuit is.

I personally began to see and view things differently in a way that helped me perceive my life through the lens of art which provided a greater and deeper meaning throughout the process in pursuing anything beyond myself. Once I began to appreciate and embrace the challenges throughout the process, it made this journey worth pursuing with everything I had. I plan to take you through the fundamental steps in understanding the process of pursuing something bigger than you, starting with my own experiences, lessons, and methods. My hope is that you will be opened up to a completely different and new perspective of life in the same way I was. Additionally, I plan to give you a completely different perspective of art, and just how significant it is in terms of pursuing something bigger than you, understanding the art that lies behind the pursuit. It is a matter of understanding the deeper meaning of art, and just how it not only changes your outlook on life but also changes the way you respond and act according to your life because art goes beyond its well-known meaning. Our life is surrounded by art that not only applies to the details of our life but more importantly, appreciating what this world around us has to offer and all the amazing things we have to offer to this world.

This process is by no means easy – it is challenging but worth it. I specially made this piece of work for people who want more out of life and who are not afraid of taking risks in becoming the best version of themselves throughout the process. If you want more than what your current state of life offers, I encourage you to really take advantage of this opportunity in helping you not only pursue something bigger than you but receiving full clarity in all the different areas of your life that is going to benefit you in so more many ways than you would have ever imagined. I say this all to let you know just how significant this is, coming from a person who is nowhere near perfect or has everything together, but instead is just a person who is desperate and willing to learn and appreciate the art in pursuing something beyond myself–a pursuit that I indeed, plan to share with you.

Chapter 1
IDENTIFIED

"The artist sees what others only catch a glimpse of."
Leonardo Da Vinci

What I find the most interesting in creating artwork is seeing other people's perspective on a piece of art. People may look at a piece artwork of mine and see one thing, while I see beyond what they see, simply because I fully understand the great significance and meaning behind the piece. People usually don't know the significance behind a piece of art, or its meaning unless they find out from the artist themselves. I truly believe that is why artist name their artwork because they're able to identify their piece of artwork based on the significance and meaning behind it. However, one will only know its true significance and meaning through the initial creator of the piece of artwork, which is the artist. The same way goes for you and I because what others see is only a glimpse compared to what our Creator sees in us. One of the most important steps in pursuing something bigger than you is understanding your identity. Who are you? Where do you come from? These are some of the most important questions we must ask ourselves in the process in order to not only understand who we really are and where we have originally come from, but to fully get a better revelation in our reason for existing and what we have to offer to the world.

Sometimes, we think we know who we are, but the truth is no one will ever know you better than the one that created you. When I say created you, I mean the one who created life from the very beginning. Don't get me wrong, the parents that gave you life will, of course, know more about you than you realize because every part of you comes from them, but your parents don't always know who you really are or know the things you were created to do. Your parents can only sometimes see what lies on the outside because they do not have the power of understanding who you truly are. However, not everyone is raised in the same environments, teachings, and lifestyles which can make it difficult in believing where you essentially come from. There are people who grow up not knowing who gave birth to them or have been mistreated their entire life, causing them to feel like their existence is a complete mistake and begin to believe that there is no better life for them based on the way they were raised and where they've come from. However, it was never intended for you to ever believe that your existence was a mistake or that your life will never get better after all that you've been through because the truth is that, your life can get better than it started once you begin to understand where you truly come from. It also goes to show that when we misunderstand where we come from, it affects the way we see ourselves, the way we live and who we become. Understanding where you come from will not only help you understand who you are, but it will give you a better understanding of why you were created the way you are, but even then, we will never really know who we are until we understand the divine source of our own being.

Divine Source

We all come from God, the Creator of all things. In fact, we bear the image of God, since God made us in His image and likeness. When I think about this, it constantly blows my mind because the way God created mankind is so significant and deep. When God created all the plants and animals around us, He spoke to a dead thing which was the dirt and spoke life into it by saying, "Let the earth bring forth the living creatures…" (Genesis 1:24), but when God created mankind, He had a completely different method. When He created mankind, He spoke to Himself when He said, "Let us make man in our image, after our likeness: and let them have dominion" (Genesis 1:26). He used the dirt from the ground to create mankind which He also breathed life into.

The fact that God had to distinguish the creation of mankind from anything else completely shows just how important and loved we are by God. God wanted to create something beyond great and worthy of loving that He made sure mankind was given His perfect essence, which means we are given the quality and resemblance of God. Although, it is often difficult to believe that we were created this way because of the things we see, come from, hear, and experience in our lives, but it is so important to never lose sight of where you originally come from. When you forget where you come from, you begin to lose sight of who you are and all that you have to offer to the world. When God created mankind, He didn't just take something out of Himself to experiment. He took something out of Him so that the thing that was in Him would manifest into something great, mighty, and powerful like Himself. When you learn to understand where you originally come from, you look at yourself differently, and in the same way, God sees you. When God looks at you, He is proud of His creation because He knows without a doubt that He has made something fearfully and wonderfully.

Redefine

There was a time when, even as a Christian, I personally struggled with my identity. Growing up, I understood that God loved me the way I was, but it was more challenging when I started to care more about the opinion of others, which led to accepting the validations from people. There were so many times in my life where I began to listen more to what people said about me instead of God's. It eventually led to the rise of insecurities I had about myself in the way God created me. I do believe, however, that everyone has their own kind of insecurities they've had to deal with in the way they were created, and my insecurities started with my body.

My childhood consisted of being very active in a lot of different sports I really enjoyed. I started competitive cheerleading at age eight and continued it until my senior year of high school. I enjoyed competitive cheerleading a lot because it was a fun but very challenging and an intense sport that kept me in the best shape of my life. However, over the years of cheering, my body began to develop differently than my peers due to the intense cardio and lifting I would do on a regular basis. I became very lean with muscle, which made me look very built all over. While it may seem like something crazy to be insecure about, I was insecure about it because of the way I was made fun of and talked about in how I was too ripped or looked like a man. There were times where I felt insecure about wearing anything that showed my arms because people would make comments about how "jacked" I was. So, it began to make me see myself differently in a way that I didn't necessarily like because I started thinking my muscles made me look manly. These kinds of thoughts would constantly run through my head all because I accepted and cared what other people thought about me. There were even times where I felt insecure about wearing a swimsuit because of how lean and tone my stomach was because I cared so much about the opinions of people when they would make comments about how my six pack was disgusting for a girl to have.

I began to not like my appearance because I would end up comparing myself to others which did no good because I began to wish I was shaped differently, all because I let people get in the way of accepting who I was and the way God created me. Over time, I had to learn how to deal with it in the right manner by focusing more on the things God says about me instead of my peers. I came to the point in my life where I began to accept who I was in God's eyes and nothing else mattered. I began to practice and learn how to be confident in who God created me to be because, regardless of my appearance, God saw way more in me than anyone ever will, and that is something that I still to this day have to remind myself of. Once I learned how to embrace my insecurities, I began to be set free from things that were once holding me back. In fact, once I fully understood my identity in God's eyes, that He has and will always be there for me because He created me in His image and likeness, I began to think differently in understanding that if He is for me, loves me and goes before me, who could possibly be against me? That is the kind of mentality I had to have in fully understanding my identity, and that is the kind of mentality that you will constantly have to practice over and over until it sticks, letting nothing get to you in the way God created you.

That was the moment I began to walk, talk, dress, and act differently and in the proper alignment with God's perspective on me. That experience changed my perspective on the purpose of insecurities–that they were created to help you build, stretch, and overcome the false accusations of your identity in order to help you become the best version of yourself! As I got older, I was thankful for the way I was built because I quickly realized how hard it is to stay in shape, and just how hard people work to get in the best shape of their life. I was also able to learn along the way how to build and stretch beyond my limits in my strength capacity, in ways I never imagined. I even eventually ended up getting involved in powerlifting at my school, that made me love getting stronger and building more muscle, helping me become the best version of myself starting with my outward appearance. Although, I constantly think back in how none of this wouldn't have been possible if I did not understand where my true identity lied. When I began to understand that my identity was found in God and who He says I am, only then was I able to constantly dwell on God's thoughts of me that overcame all the lies that tried to make me lose sight of who I was. What I want you to understand is just how significant it is in understanding who God says you are because only then will you be able to face and overcome any insecurities that begin to rise from the opinions of others. Never let the validations of other people define who you really are because God made no mistake in creating His masterpiece. Learning to become confident in who God says you are, will eventually lead you into becoming more confident in who you are in such a way that insecurities are nothing but beneath you. Your self-esteem changes in such a way that you are able to live without the fear and validations that tried to destroy you, you can fully stand firm and full of confidence in your true identity because you understand that your true identity and value lies in the most divine source of all, God Himself.

Masterpiece

Not every piece of artwork is considered a masterpiece simply because there are certain pieces of artwork an artist must create in order to master the skill. It takes time to master anything; in fact, it requires practice and patience. A masterpiece will always standout compared to the rest because the skill of the artist has been mastered enough to fulfill the overall quality of a piece. The masterpieces we know of today such as the *Mona Lisa*, goes down as one of the highest insurance value for a painting in all of history, that is worth $100 million as of 2018. A masterpiece like that, of course, would be so valuable and expensive because of the time and effort put into something for it to become a masterpiece. The same way goes for God when He was in the process of creating mankind. We are His masterpiece that took time to master, starting with creating everything around us. When you start to understand that you are a masterpiece in God's eyes, you begin to understand where your value comes from.

Regardless of anything difficult you've had to put up with your entire life in not accepting the way you were created, based on what people say about you, I want to let you know that when God sees you, He sees His masterpiece, that He loves, cherishes, and takes full pride in. You are worthy and loved beyond measures, and I hope you will always remember that, especially the next time people try to tear you down in the way God created you to be. Understand that any of the insecurities that you have is essentially a form of art that has not been mastered because it takes time, but you will get there by embracing who you are in all that God has created you to be. You are perfect the way you are because God created you and He is a master of His work, so whatever

He creates, words will never be able to describe the beauty and essence of His work.

Hand and hand

It is truly all about understanding the divine source in which you were created that begins to change the way you see and accept things around you. Once you are able to accept your identity in who you are in God's eyes, it will only then lead you to the discovery of understanding the reason for your existence. You began to learn that everything from the way you were raised in certain environments, lifestyles, your difficulties, and insecurities has everything to not only deal with who God created you to become, but also dealing with everything in helping you understand what you were created to do on this earth. Only then have you taken the first step in pursuing something bigger than you, with the great work of art that lies in your true identity that begins to reveal a greater purpose and meaning of your life.

"Until you cross the bridge of your insecurities, you can't begin to explore your possibilities." -Tim Fargo

Chapter 2
Why Me?

"Whatever you were born to do, you were built with." - Myles Munroe

An artist doesn't necessarily become an artist because they were just born that way; they eventually had to discover the creative skill that was placed down on the inside of them over time. Once an artist understands who they are because of what is put on the inside of them, they began to understand the reason for their existence. When you begin to see yourself in the way God originally planned for you too, you begin to get a glimpse of what is placed down on the inside of you. God reveals things to us like no one ever will because He knows every single detail about us. He only knows the things we were created to do on this earth, regardless of what others say. We often live in a society today that constantly convinces us of the things we were created to do, when in reality it was never meant for us, according to God's plan for our lives. We will often make the mistake of looking for things around us to make us feel useful and meaningful in this life when in reality, it all starts with what is deep down within us. I've noticed in my generation particularly that we often try to live our lives based on the influencers of our pop culture, in regard to their opinions, lifestyles, images or interests.

We sometimes make the mistake in trying to become something God never had in mind or try to live up to people's expectations. When things like this occur, things become less unique and original, all because we made the mistake in being anything but ourselves. However, everyone is already unique and original in their own way. It is something to be proud and grateful for because God took the time to make you uniquely designed like no other human being on earth, and He has specifically placed something down on the inside of you that no one else has because it is unique, original and built in you. When you begin to not primarily seek the influencers of this world, but seek the One who knows everything about you, only then will we begin to discover things in you like never before. God has specifically placed something deep down within you for a specific purpose. The fact that you are still breathing is evidence that God is not done with you and is just waiting for you to discover that thing that He has placed within you. However, it is so important to understand the significance of the special and unique thing that He has placed down on the inside of you, because it is the one thing God designed and created you to master and do magnificently well at, like no one else. What God has placed down on the inside of you is not just the only thing He just created for you to dominate, but essentially a way for Him to use you in ways He sees fit, in order to bless you beyond measures, so that you would become a blessing to those around you, starting with the significant thing that lies down on the inside of you.

Although, it is also important that once you begin to get a glimpse of what God has placed down on the inside of you, don't abandon it. There are times in our lives where we begin to doubt and question ourselves in the things we can do and have to offer to the world all because we never fully acknowledged the thing God has placed down on the inside of us. No matter how small or big the thing may seem that God has placed down on the inside of you, it will never be able to measure up to your expectations, instead go beyond them. In the same way, a tree is formed, it starts as a seed, and when it is placed into the ground, all we see is nothing but a seed. However, when God sees that seed, He automatically sees a tree because He only knows what that seed is capable of becoming and its significant purpose. You look at a seed and that is all that you see, but as time goes by, you begin to see it grow into something much greater and bigger than it originally started. That is the way God uses our lives in placing something down on the inside of us that may, in the beginning, begin as something small and simple, but to God, it is something beyond what we could ever think or imagine. The greatest part of it all is that while God may place something down on the inside of us, it grows beyond our expectations to the point where we begin to see a harvest of all the things that started with that one little thing God placed within us. It all starts with the discovering of what God has placed down on the inside of you, regardless of who you are or what you have been through, God chose you. You have no idea what that thing down on the inside of you is truly capable of until you find out.

Beauty in Brokenness

While it may sound great in understanding that God has placed something down on the inside of you, it may be something difficult to accept because you may have doubts in thinking that there's no way God could possibly place something down on the inside of someone like you. The truth is, regardless of who you are, the things you've done or things you have been raised around, God knew you way before it all and still decided to place something so special on the inside of you. It is important to understand that no one is perfect or will ever be more perfect than God. We all go through difficult situations in our lives that we have no control over that often leaves us feeling broken in different areas of our lives. Although, what I can say is that from my own personal experiences in feeling broken in areas of my life, God was actually able to reveal the significance of being broken. Brokenness means experiencing loss of hope, where we feel defeated and torn apart. No one wants to experience any kind of brokenness in their life, but in reality, we often experience times of brokenness no matter how hard we try to avoid it.

The feeling of being broken comes from so many things in our lives whether that means experiencing times of being mistreated, rejected, deeply hurt, betrayed or depressed. I've personally learned that it doesn't matter who you are, you will always experience some kind of brokenness in your life, but it is a matter of how you deal with it and who you become from it. I personally experience moments in my life where I struggled with feeling lonely, rejected and hurt throughout my life. Growing up I was very sigh and passive, making it difficult to make friends because I always wanted to please everyone without hurting them, which in the end just lead to my friendship being taken advantage of. What I did not realize is the hurt and betrayal that came along with doing everything in my power to please the people I cared so much for, but I eventually had to understand and learn what true friendship is and who real friends are. I eventually had to learn to stand my ground in order to protect myself and not let others walk over me like I was nothing, which of course was not something easy for me because I wasn't the best at speaking my mind. However, I would constantly be faced with the idea that no one truly cared about who I was, only what I could offer. I faced times of always feeling lonely even in the midst of having lots of friends from school and extracurricular activities, all because very few understood or accepted me for who I really was.

I did notice that I was indeed a lot different than my peers and had different interest, which was the reason I would feel rejected at times because I never could fit in. I even began to think that there was something wrong with me all because no one fully understood me or the things I had a big interest in. I cried so many times during times of feeling lonely because I began to feel like no one truly wanted to be my friend, and began to lose hope in finding true friends. In those moments of feeling completely worthless, I would constantly turn to God for comfort and healing. What I did not realize was I did not only had God to watch over me and comfort me through it all, but I also had the closest true friends right by my side all these years, who accepted me for who I was and loved me unconditionally, my parents. Only then God was able to show me just how much I needed Him in the midst of everything, in order to reveal to me that I was never alone and that He already placed one of the biggest blessings in my life.

I learned throughout that process that God uses the brokenness in us for a specific reason in building us to become all that He has created us to be. God can only build on things that are broken, so everything we personally experience in our lives in regards to feeling broken is just a great way for God to reveal Himself to us in a way like never before, which only then He is able to build and establish us. You see, part of the reason we experience any form of brokenness in our life is to understand that we do not have the ability or power to fix the brokenness in us, leaving us to turn to the one who can. We often mistake the purpose behind our lives in the moments of feeling completely defeated, worthless, and lost, when God purposely created it to be a time of building and establishing the strong and conqueror He has created you to be. You would truly be surprised by the things God can do through brokenness, by elevating, positioning, promoting, and truly putting you in the right place He had planned for you all along. The most beautiful part of it all is while you feel broken in the different areas of your life, God does it purposely not to break you or destroy you, but to build you with Grace. His Grace is sufficient and mightily powerful to do things your eyes have not seen, starting with the things that have hurt you, made you feel worthless, inferior, alone, ashamed, forgotten, betrayed or lost.

The moments of brokenness we often deal with has so much to do with who we chose to become during the process. This is because it is also a choice on whether or not you are going to let the things and people of this world get to you in such a way that begins to destroy who you are and break you into pieces. It's about understanding how to deal with your brokenness in the right manner to where only God is able to do His mighty work within you, to where He is able to do things beyond your expectations.

You see, there are lots of broken people in our world today who constantly hurt and morn over things that have happened in the past, but chose not to move forward and dwell on the thought of thinking and believing that they're always going to feel and be in that current condition for the rest of their life. However, the truth of the matter is that if you ever want more out of what your current state of life has to offer, you have to learn how to push forward and move on no matter how much it hurts because if you continue to stay where you are hurting and mourning, you'll never go any farther and time will continue to fly by. If you choose to let your past or your current conditions and circumstances rob you of peace, joy, happiness and the fullness of life, you will constantly live miserable all because you have refused to change your mind and take action in your life.

The thing is, as long as you stay where you are, with the same mindset, you'll never go any further because until you learn to let things go in regards to your past or current condition in life, you will never grow. If you never learn how to grow from the things you have been through or have constantly faced within your life, you will never be able to become the best version of yourself in which God created you to be. In fact, if you never put in the effort in developing the best version of yourself, you'll never be able to pursue the things beyond you, because one of the biggest things it requires is courage, and when you can develop the courage to deal and move past the brokenness that you've had to deal with in your life, only then are you given a great opportunity in beginning to walk into the great fullness of life without the shame, guilt, and unforgiveness that keep up hostage. The only way you will be able to move forward is by being able to accept your brokenness and being able to let go and let God handle it, in building you and preparing you for what lies ahead. In fact, if you never really go through anything tough, you'll never really grow, or be prepared for the things in which God has in store for you.

Brokenness is just a way to break you down in certain areas in your life where God is then able to evaluate and establish you in ways like never before, revealing the true you. I've personally learned myself that further down the line, the brokenness I dealt with in my life had everything to do with me becoming who God created me to be, that only then began to reveal the real me and the purpose behind my existence. There are some things we must experience in regards to feeling broken that often leads to us figuring out why we had to go through such a difficult time in our lives. One of the biggest things God likes to do is challenge us with feeling broken in moments of our life so that we become desperate and willing to reach out to Him for help when we understand we can no longer do it ourselves. When we receive the help we need in moments of feeling broken, only then is God able to reveal to us the purpose behind it all and began to give us a different perspective on what brokenness is. You will begin to understand that all the times of feeling broken in your life was always there to purposely benefit you for your own good, in helping you grow and blossom throughout life, not destroy you. You begin to view the pain and suffering you go through as another way of being evaluated in your life in becoming the best version of yourself. You began to understand the purpose behind the pain and suffering that may have put you in difficult situations in your life, but in the end, it was all for a greater purpose in helping you not only become the best version of yourself, but reveal to you that you were just a step closer in pursuing something beyond you.

> *"The Lord is close to the brokenhearted and saves those who are crushed in spirit." -Psalms 34:18*

Conqueror

When you begin to understand the pain you've felt in moments of feeling broken, your perspective is opened up into a great discovery. Only then, God begins to reveal to you the bits and pieces of your life that has so much to do with your purpose. There is always a greater purpose behind any kind of pain you will ever have to deal with in your life, it a matter of understanding how you choose to deal with it, by letting your pain become your prison or your platform in which God uses to build you up. However, once you begin to accept the moments of brokenness you've had to deal with in your life, you begin to realize that everything you ever went through was never meant to destroy you, but build you in understanding your true identity, that you are a conqueror. Growing up, English was one of my least favorite subjects because it was something I always struggle with, especially when it came to comprehension and or simply reading books since I hated reading. I wasn't very good at writing as well, because I struggled with grammar and spelling all the time. There were so many times where I felt like a complete failure and loser to those around me because I had trouble pronouncing words and ended up getting made fun of. However, I began to reach a point where I was so fed up with it; I became determined to find ways to improve, which resulted in me trying to read more books that interest me and began writing down my prayers as a way to improve in my writing skills.

I never realized how much I would improve if I hadn't given up and let the little things get to me. If I had not tried at all in improving in the area of my life where I felt the most defeated, I wouldn't have discovered my love for reading books and writing. See, I quickly learned in that moment that the things that made me feel stupid, worthless, and ashamed of myself eventually would become something that worked out in my favor for good. It's in these moments where you need to understand and identify the things in your life that you constantly wrestle with, in order to find ways to improve in that area to where the struggles, disappointments, or brokenness have no choice but to serve you in your favor in becoming all that God created you to be. I even think to myself now that if I had not faced the things that caused me so much disappointment in my life, I would've never caught myself discovering a passion that was hidden in me or understand how this would eventually have to deal with the bits and pieces of my purpose in life. I think back to the old me, and I would have never imagined I would end up writing a book one day. I never realized that the pain and hardships that I faced would not only lead me into discovering the unknown passions within me, but also end up offering me so much more than I imagined. If I had given up on even trying to find ways to get better at the one thing I truly wasn't good at, I wouldn't be where I am today.

There are moments in our life when we get to a point where we want to give up because nothing seems to go in our favor no matter how hard we try. However, In these moments, you begin to lose hope and give up, thinking that the one thing you've been working so hard for isn't for you, but in reality, it has always been the thing that was going to shape you into being the best version of you. See, God would never place something on you if He knew you couldn't handle it, so even in the times you began to feel like a complete failure, God still sees so much more and in fact, watches how you respond to the mistakes and failures you face. Our failure is simply a test of our character because, in those moments of failure, it reveals who we are, what we do, and who we become. See, the truth is, failure is a way of life, and the only way to succeed is to fail because, without failure, you miss out on the levels of growth, experiences, and lessons failure has to offer, which in the end only leads to true success. It is a matter of understanding that the things that you have found the most difficult in your life were never meant to tear down who you are as a person, instead give you opportunities to conquer the things that constantly tried to defeat you from the beginning. It is one of the most beneficial things in life that will help you pursue something bigger than yourself once you understand that you have the ability to conquer the things life throws your way. In fact, God made it known that "in all these things we are more than conquerors through Him who loved us". (Romans 8:37)

CHAPTER 3
THE VISION

"A vision is not a picture of what could be; it is an appeal to our better selves, a call to become something more."
-Rosabeth Moss Kanter

    Behind every piece of artwork lies a powerful, detailed and structured vision. Art wouldn't be what it is if vision did not exist. However, you may be thinking of vision in terms of sight, but art lies in the visions of the unseen. You see, an artist's piece of work comes from vision, where they have a vision and put in the work to see the vision come to pass in order to share with the world. The same thing applies in our own lives in many different ways in becoming something we have always dreamed of being or doing. For us to even vision something, it all starts with a thought that is placed within us. We first think of something that we may want to be or do only to find ourselves fantasizing and dreaming on the thought, making the mistake of misunderstanding what a vision really is. However, it is important to understand the difference between a vision and a dream because while they both seem similar, they are indeed not the same thing.

    A dream is something you can dwell on that you wish and hope to see, but has the chance of changing over time. A vision is a vivid picture of the unseen of something that produces direction and purpose in someone's life. While both have the idea in visually picturing something, they, in fact, go hand and hand in creating the desired outcome. See, dreams and visions work better together when they are planned, positioned, and persistent. While it may be easy to dream, it is another thing to have a vision, which is why there has to be a plan behind any kind of dream, worth working and fighting for. However, just planning ways to see your dream come to pass is not enough because behind every plan requires work and a great challenge. It is simply about being able to prepare yourself for the things you must do and the things that come as a surprise in helping you achieve the dream. In terms of things coming at you by surprise, it can quickly become something that gets in the way of fulfilling your dream, which is usually a test to see whether or not it is a real dream and whether or not there is a real vision behind it. If you are not able to face whatever comes your way in the midst of everything in terms of striving towards your dream due to the lack of persistence, then you may want to reevaluate the dream and vision. It is important to stay persistent throughout the process because you not only become a real dreamer, but you become a doer of your dreams, requiring you to face the challenges and put in the hard work in aiming towards the vision, that you refuse to let anything get in the way of, especially when it comes to your sight.

Sight

One of the most difficult things faced in times of striving and aiming towards your vision is the presence of sight. Sight often makes it difficult at times to persevere in the moments where we want to give up. See, sight is the thing in which we can see with our very own eyes, making it harder to stay focused on the vision. See, although you might have had a vivid vision of what you want to do or become 10 years from now, it is hard to see it come to pass when you look at your current state of life. You may not be happy at all with where you are or what things you have done up until this point of your life, but the importance of it all is not to let your current circumstances change the way you initially vision yourself. Of course, it's hard, but it's truly about holding on tight to what is true to you, regardless of the situations you face throughout the process.

I'll never forget the first time I received glasses; it was literary a life-changing moment for me. It was like for the longest time; I could not see clearly, all because I did not have very good eyesight. Although, the moment I put on my glasses for the first time, they took me outside to test them out and I was amazed by what I had seen. In that moment, I had a completely different perspective of life and just how much detail there was in everything that I saw around me. Once I was able to receive a perfect vision, I began to look at things so differently in a way that made me understand the significance of being able to see clearly. It is initially the same way we use our eyesight each and every day of our life. In fact, not everyone is born with perfect eyesight, but that doesn't mean someone with bad eyesight can't receive 20/20 vision. However, not having great eyesight can be seen in a very similar situation in terms of dealing with the difficult circumstances we face right in front of us every day that often clouds our desired vision. While some enjoy the circumstances that they are faced with right before their eyes, others can't bear to stand another moment of the tough circumstances they have to face. There are real people who go through really tough situations in their life that they sometimes have no control over, and what eventually ends up happening is that their sight begins to be clouded by the judgment, failure, shame, brokenness and negativity that appears right before their eyes. The thing is we often make the mistake in letting the things that are in our sight define who we are, what we can do, or who we can become when in reality God never insisted it to be that way. The truth of the matter is that there are going to be things in our life that we can't stand to see happen right before us, but that doesn't mean we can't change it. However, it is important to understand the right procedures in changing your sight to serve your vision.

1. **Dwelling Gratitude**

   One of the most important things to understand during the process of changing the way you see and handle the circumstances you are facing is to understand the significance of dwelling on gratitude. Regardless of what you are facing that is difficult and seems as if it is something that you can no longer bear, you must dwell on the things in which you are grateful for. While it seems like it is something that isn't effective, I promise you that this is a great step in changing your perspective of life, coming from someone who had to learn how to do this themselves. You have to begin to train your mind to dwell on the right things even in the midst of everything that seems to be going wrong. Start with looking at the positives even if it seems small. For example, I just received my grade for a class that was difficult, in which I worked hard to maintain a B and up, however when I saw the final grade for the course it was a 79.64. In this moment, I am frustrated and very upset because I was not able to receive my desired grade for the course, so naturally, I began to worry and think of all the negative things on how it is going to bring down my GPA and so on.

Although, I had to take a moment and realize that my sight was beginning to be clouded by my disappointment, so then I had to take a moment and dwell on the positives. I started off by telling myself that it is not the end of the world for me, that I should be grateful to be living and even more grateful to have the opportunity to attend college. I also had to dwell on the fact that my grades do not define who I am or my worth. See, what we often end up taking advantage of in the midst of our failures and disappointments in life are the simplest things that we should be grateful for. You see, while you may think you may be going through one of the toughest situations in your life, you don't even think for a moment on how someone else would rather be in the situation that you are facing than their very own. What you must understand in any given difficult moment of your life is that things could be far worse than they already are, and some of the little things we complain and get upset about don't even compare to the things in which other people have to put up with every day of their lives. Learning to be thankful for the simplest things in our lives does great measures in taking your mind off the things that have hurt you, disappointed you, or caused you to lose hope in your past. You begin to stop dwelling on the present and begin to move towards the future. One of the things I personally believe we should constantly dwell on in the midst of anything that comes our way is understanding the significance of gratitude in any given moment.

You must understand that you have to learn to develop the mindset that may say 'yes my life is a complete mess but I am still breathing and living and as long as I am breathing and living, God is not finished with me yet'. When you learn and practice this method, you will not only begin to see your circumstances have no power over you, but you will begin to not just go through things, but grow through them. When you begin to grow in your gratitude of all that life has to offer, you not only become a more positive person, but your attitude begins to grow as well. As my dad would say, "Gratitude becomes the altitude of your attitude", meaning that the more grateful and thankful you are for even the little things, the greater attitude you will have on life even in the midst of trials and tribulations. In fact, this method not only can help with your current situations and conditions in life, but it, more importantly, reveals to God the kind of stewardship you have with your gratitude. The more grateful you are the more God is able to continue blessing you. There lies great power in gratitude, for it leaves no room for negativity or complaining because you begin to recognize and understand that you have so much to be thankful for even in the smallest things.

2. Catch the L

The next step requires you to take the lost, in terms of willing to accept the L. This process is all about learning how to train your mind during the disappointing times of your life, to accept your losses as lessons. Maybe you didn't get what you wanted out of the situation, but by using the dwelling gratitude, you are grateful for the little things that made a big difference, and since you have come to terms with yourself in accepting the loss, you've also learned some valuable lessons. You learn lessons in terms of things that you can improve on, avoid or better prepare yourself for the next time. While we make catching an L seem so bad, in reality, it's a win because you learn and grow from your mistakes and disappointments. Once I took that big fat L in receiving a C in the class and focused my attention on the more important things I had to be grateful for, I was ready to move on.

In fact, I learned a few lessons in understanding that the next time I am faced with a difficult class, I am going to have to go the extra mile in my studying and preparation so that I leave myself very little room to be disappointed in the end. Now, I can confidently say that I see all my L's as dubs because I chose to learn from my mistakes and disappointments rather than let them defeat me. I personally believe deep down in my heart that you can do the same because God takes so much pride in who you are and because God created you. He designed you to succeed simply because your success has and will always be in God's best interest. However, success is the result of the decisions we make, so it starts with you making the decisions in your life that determines how successful you become, starting with your mentality. I truly believe you have the kind of mentality to fail because it is what serves you to succeed, knowing that when things don't go as planned, you lose something, or make a bad decision, it all comes down to the way you chose to perceive yourself in terms of your failure. It's about making a conscious decision on whether or not you let failure become the thing that stops you when it is purposely created to push you and test you. Success lies on the other side of failure, so until you fail, only then will you see the other side of success because you've chosen not to give up, but persevere. Success starts with failure, and until you are able to accept and move forward from the mistakes and disappointments that have happened in your life, you will always stays where you started. It is truly about understanding that while you may not have complete control over the things that happen in your life, you do however have control over your attitude, mind, and thoughts during the process. That is why I encourage you to have a completely different perspective on losses that your losses are made to serve and benefit you, not defeat you or tear you down. What I personally believe is the best thing of all is the fact that once you are able to take the L and move on, you begin to let nothing stop you or cloud your sight in the vision you have created for yourself.

3. Write It

Once you receive a vision that is vivid and clear in the things you plan and hope to see come to pass in your life, WRITE IT DOWN! I can't even stress this enough in how significant this step is, because it is the stepping stone in creating the life you have desired. This step is so important because only then are you writing down the things unseen. In fact, God makes it known through His Word in just how important a simple step like this is when He says, "write down this vision, and make it plain upon tables, that he may run that readeth it." (Habakkuk 2:2). This simply means that once we receive the vision, it is important that we write it down immediately and make it known so that each and every day of our lives, we have something to constantly glance at as we run our race in the things we strive and pursue in this life. I want you to catch just how important this is because it has so much to do in pursuing something bigger than you! Writing down your vision is a lot deeper than you think because just think about the Bible, for instance, everything is written, but before it was written, it came from a vision, God's vision from the very beginning of life to the end. This should show you just how powerful and meaningful it is to write down your vision because it gives life to certain things that have yet to happen, in the same way, God's Word gives life, direction, and guidance.

See, the big thing I also want you to see is how God used ordinary, imperfect people to place a strong, vivid vision in them that they would eventually end up writing down that would manifest into something much greater than they ever imagined. However, before you write down the vision, you need to identify whether or not it is a legit vision. The best way to test your vision is by making sure it's impossible to do in your current state of mind because, if it is even slightly possible in the current state of mind or condition you're in, well, it's probably just a goal. See, the big thing I want you to understand in terms of a vision is that you will never be able to see it come to pass by your own ability because it requires a divine power source, and a vision is something you work towards that has levels and levels to it, not just something you just accomplish. As you work in the direction of your vision, there are going to be things you will accomplish along the way that began to set the foundation and next steps in seeing the vision fully manifested. A vision has so much tied into it, which is why you must write it down so that it never leaves you and you are constantly reminded of it each and every day of your life.

4. By Faith

This important step is the determining factor of everything in terms of your vision. See, one of the most important things a vision requires is faith, because without faith the vision begins to perish. faith is the one thing that is going to help endure the vision and make it come to pass. In fact, faith has so much to do with vision because it is the substance of things hoped for and the evidence of things not seen. Faith and vision go hand-in-hand because they are both an essence of things sight cannot comprehend. It's the same way with God, He isn't something we can necessarily see, but only through His Word that is written we are able to gain knowledge, wisdom, and faith in understanding who He is. However, we receive faith through believing in the unseen, which seems hard and confusing but what God likes to do is reveal to us what faith is when we simply learn how to believe. Once we learn how to believe in the unseen and see those things happen right before our eyes, only then do we begin to experience the power in faith. I will never forget the moment in my life where I experienced faith in God like no other that made what seemed impossible,

possible right before my very own eyes. In 2015, it was my first year being on one of the most decorated medium, coed all-star cheerleading teams in the world.

This was the team I worked so hard to be placed on, and the moment I was placed on this team, it was a dream come true because it marked the first time I would finally get the chance to attend the Cheerleading World Championships, which was what I constantly dreamed and worked years to get too. However, it became one of the most devastating moments of my life because my team put on an unforgettable performance that was overlooked and caused us to receive a 2nd place, when deep down, there was no doubt, we were going to become the 2015 World Champions. However, life happens, and in the end, it turned out to not be our year. I honestly never cried so hard in my life until that very moment, seeing everything I worked so extremely hard for, with everything I had given and sacrificed over the years, just completely crumble into pieces. There were even moments where I didn't understand why God let something like this happen to me, after my prayers and everything He did for me in helping me get where I was, in that very moment, I even began to lose faith in God in the things He could do in my life. However, I've never been the kind of person to give up on something I really wanted, so the following year, I had a completely different mindset and vision for myself, considering it was the beginning of the new year as a team and without a doubt, I believed that we would be the 2016 World Champions. I began to do things differently in not fully giving up on God, after everything He had done in my life. I made the decision that God was going to be a part of everything that I was trying to accomplish going forward, letting Him have complete control of everything.

Fast forward, I was attending my second Worlds, and I knew that all the extra hard work my team and I put in was not going to be for nothing this year. I even felt called to share encouraging words to my teammates that would help us in the process because I learned quickly that we couldn't do this alone, we needed God to have His way in making it all possible. We put on a great performance, but there was just a minor mistake that would cause us everything in becoming the next World Champions. In that moment, I fell completely apart once again because it truly felt like nothing was working and God didn't hear me out or my prayers. In this very moment, I began to lose faith again in the one thing that constantly keeps me strong and moving which was God. I remember sitting there with my team during awards feeling anxious and beyond nervous, but there was just something that constantly told me not to give up and have faith, that keeps me believing in the little faith I had at the moment.

They were about to announce the 2nd place team, and this was going to be the deal breaker in whether or not we would leave as World Champions or not. However, what I would like to point out is the fact that everyone knew about the minor mistake that happened in our routine and already knew that our chances were over. When I tell you what great things can happen in your life when you walk by faith and not by sight, it will truly change your entire life for the better. In 2016, my team: Spirit of Texas Medium Coed was announced as the new World Champions. In that moment, I received a level of faith like no other that I had no idea would change the rest of my life. In the midst of the disappointment and doubts, there was something in me that refused to give in to losing my faith in God and His promise. Even when everyone doubted my team and said that there was no way it was going to happen, God showed up and made a way out of no way, showing me right in that very moment the importance of having faith and what great things can manifest from it. I think back now in how I can constantly share this great testimony and get a new revelation every time in how God used one of the things I had such a great love and passion for, to completely reveal Himself to me, showing me the great power that lies within Him when I learn to have complete trust and faith in Him to do the impossible in my life. I tell you this personal experience to show you the power of faith, that when you begin to have faith in God to do the impossible things in your life, regardless of your current condition, He will make it happen only if you do not lose faith in your vision and what He has promised you. For God makes it clear and precise in His Word when He says, "Truly I say to you, whoever says to this mountain, 'be taken up and cast into the sea,' and does not doubt in his heart, but believes that what he says will happen, it will be granted him." (Matthew 11:23).

5. **Execute**

Last but not least, is the final step in seeing your sight serve your vision, which is one of the most important, executions. While a vision requires faith, faith requires work because faith without works is dead. You can't have faith in something and not exercise it, because it requires work. I firmly believe that some of the reasons I may have not received God's promise the first time in my desire to become a World Champion, was simply because He first and foremost wanted me to have complete trust and faith in Him in making it possible and secondly, He wanted to teach me valuable lessons along the process of learning how to exercise my faith by executing the things that were going to help make it happen, starting with Him alone. Once we understand the things in which we are grateful for in helping us accept the failures in our life and persevere, walking by faith and not by sight, only then are we going to be able to put the actual work into the things we want to see come to pass in our lives. It's in the same way a person is a dreamer, but for that dream to become a reality, they must be a doer. Execution is very beneficial when it comes to seeing your vision happen right before your eyes because you finally have something in life that you are working towards. In fact, since you have a clear, vivid vision, your decisions are based on your vision. It becomes a deciding factor in certain situations on whether or not this is going to hurt my vision or push it to the next level. When we think in terms of vision, it becomes the determining factor for all the ways we chose to live our life. You begin to learn along the way, what things are good and bad for your vision in terms of whether it is certain people, habits or even your mindset. The big thing is understanding how important your vision is to you and understanding what things must be done in order to protect it at all cost.

Outsight

When it comes to our sight, it is so important to understand how to use our outsight. Outsight is the ability to see beyond who you are as a person and your perspective. This is why I list these 5 fundamental tools in helping you develop an outsight that will change your perspective on life and change your current condition of sight to serve your vision in the end. However, these changes have everything to do with your mindset and very little to do with changing the amazing person God has already created. I make that clear because of what I've noticed in my generation personally, is just how much we belittle the value that is on the inside and outside of us. There are some of us who are not happy with what we see in the mirror, so we constantly strive to be anyone else but ourselves. It is why identity is truly one of the most important factors in the way we choose to live our lives because, it is essentially the source in which all things come from in revealing our true self. In fact, I make this statement because if you do not know who you really are, you'll do anything. However, we live in a generation now where we pay so much attention to the things on the outside of us, thinking it adds value to us because of the price, when in reality, the real value lies within. You see, there are things within us that are priceless, like love for instance, because it is simply something you can't buy. Although, real love may come at a cost, but it isn't something money can buy because where there is real love, there is a sacrifice that is forever priceless.

What we often overlook is the fact that the essence for our living is nothing but love because it cost the sacrifice of God's only son to die for our sins so that we could have everlasting life. The point that I am trying to make clear is that you were already born with so much value on you and inside of you that you don't have to find value in the materialistic things of this world just to feel valued. If anything, the material things and adjustments are just to add to the value that is already on the inside and outside of you, for it does not define who you really are. It is important to point out that no matter what you look like, you are God's creation and because we come from a perfect God, we receive the same essence in being perfectly made through Him. We often, will make the mistake in changing certain things about us that God purposely placed on the outside of us to embrace that initially makes you unique and different in every possible way.

Never let your current condition of sight get to you, causing you to misinterpret the things in which God purposely placed within you or on you to embrace because, little do you realize that the things that cause you to see yourself differently than God and finding ways to find value, are ways that start to make you drift away from the great vision God has placed within you. When we begin to live our lives according to the visions, plans, and dreams that God deposits within us, it is extremely important to understand that there are going to be things that constantly try to get in the way and stop us from pursuing the great things beyond ourselves. It is why you must develop the greatest contributors when it comes to pursuing anything bigger than yourself, starting with your focus and discipline.

Chapter 4
PRODUCT OF FOCUS & DISCIPLINE

"If you want to be disciplined in any area of your life, stay focused exclusively on the outcome you want." - Joe Duncan

An artist's work is solely determined by their sense of focus and discipline. While an artist starts with a vision, it isn't enough to just execute the things in which needs to be done in order for the vision to come to life. See, the artist has to develop a mentality that is focused on the desired outcome that requires them to be disciplined throughout the process. This, believe it or not, is the big deal breaker for everything in pursuing something bigger than you. You can have a vision and plan, but if you do not have the mentality of being focused and making yourself disciplined, then your chances of doing or being anything beyond you are far from it. In fact, learning to become focused on the things you want to see in your life is not easy, because it requires some serious work in making sure you constantly have the right mindset at all times.

Staying focus on the vision sounds easy, but it is a completely different approach with expectations you must be willing to accept in order to see your desired outcome -

an approach that requires you to become very careful in the way you manage your time. Time is all we have nowadays, and it is our responsibility to take advantage of the time we have to become or do things that are yet to be discovered. See, while you can lose money and eventually get it back, time, on the other hand, works differently because it is something that we cannot get back. One of the greatest things about time is how no matter how wealthy or poor, sick or healthy, young or old you are, every single one of us gets the same amount of time each and every day. However, it is a matter of how we use our time that determines the course of our life. The last thing you want to do is waste the precious time you have here on earth when there is so much that God has placed within you that requires the time and effort to discover and develop it. The big point that I am trying to make is how significant it is to learn how to be a good steward in your time by staying focused. The thing that I personally wouldn't want you to do is to look back at the course of your life and realize all the time and opportunities you missed out on, all because of your lack of focus. However, what I do want you to understand is that it's never too late, no matter who you are or how old you are, it is never too late to pursue the things that are beyond you. The real question is whether or not you are up for a challenge?

Think

Where it all begins lies in the way you think, because your focus is a product of what you think. We often, don't even realize the impact the way we think has on our lives. In fact, it is often the deciding factor in the way we carry ourselves, our actions and is initially a big part of who we become. However, it's about understanding that the way you think is powerful and can also be dangerous. Thoughts usually come from the things we see and hear, so whether or not the things we hear are positive or negative, it will eventually determine our thought process in the way we live our life. Think about a kid who has grown up being told he is a failure, since he is constantly being told this, it eventually becomes something he thinks and believes about himself. This is a prime example in how the things we begin to hear, begin to perceive the things we think and believe about ourselves, that can be dangerous, causing a great impact on the course of our life. Although, it's difficult because it is not like you can control the things people say about you, but you can develop a way that filters the things that are positive and more beneficial to you, such as selective hearing.

Selective hearing is one of the most helpful things you can learn to practice in terms of protecting your vision and your thinking process. I've personally had to learn for myself how to use selective hearing when it comes to me staying focused on my vision and the right thoughts about myself. Selective hearing is very important because it basically gives you a way to filter the things you hear. For instance, I like to use selective hearing when I know I am going to be talking to certain people who usually have nothing positive to say or find ways to talk down on me. I personally found this to be the best method for me in terms of being respectful, polite and friendly, all at the same time. However, I want to point out that this method is not as easy as it seems because, it requires you to be truly confident in who you are and who God says you are. Only then, will you know what to truly think and believe about yourself, that will eventually overcome everything that is said about you that isn't true based on the things you know and think about yourself. This method requires practice because you have to learn how to focus on the things that are true and the things in which God says about you, instead of the false opinions people make about you. Once you are able to develop the method of selective hearing, only then will you begin to see things much clearly in dwelling on the things that are true about you. It even helps increase your self-esteem and confidence because you begin to become more confident in who you are, that every false opinion or insult completely phases you. You are also able to move forward in staying focused on your vision and the things you wish to see come to pass.

Distraction

One of the biggest challenges faced during the process of being focused is distractions. Distractions are purposely made to stop or delay the things in which you are working towards. Distractions, however, come in many shapes and sizes according to our everyday lives, whether it's certain things or people. If you're ever going to become focused on certain things in your life that are going to help you pursue something beyond you, it important to understand how to handle distractions in the right manner. The way you deal with distractions is by letting your vision become stronger than the things that constantly try to stir you away from the vision you have for your life. You have to be serious about your vision to the point where you have no choice but to avoid distractions. What I've personally learned from distractions myself is just how much time they take away from the opportunities and things that primarily needed my focus and time more than anything. However, the hardest part of it all is being able to identify the things in our life that in reality are distractions.

As I said, if you are serious about your vision, the easiest way to identify distractions in your life is through observation. The observation involves a very important question in asking whether or not this thing or person in my life is helping me make progress in achieving my vision or are they causing me to drift away from it? Although, like I said, if you are for real about achieving your vision and determined to stay focused along the way, this is a step you have to be willing to take. The truth is that not everything in life is easy, so it is important that we become reasonable with the decisions and choices we make in regards to living the life we have desired for ourselves. I'm being completely honest when I say this was one of the hardest things for me to do because I knew how easy it was for me to get distracted especially because of the kind of person I am. To give you a brief story with one of the biggest distractions I had to deal with in different seasons of my life, it was boys. The idea of being in a relationship had always seemed like something I wanted, especially during the times when some of my peers were in relationships. In fact, it was one thing I found myself struggling with because while I was in school trying to stay focused on my academics and achievements in sports, it often, would always cross my mind in wanting to talk to someone who had interest in me.

Although, because I would always follow up my parent's advice, I would always be told just to stay focused and keep it moving. In those times, of course, it didn't always seem like the best advice until I better understood it as I got older. I got older; I also became more ambitious in the things I wanted out of my life, so I had no choice but to become more focused. That was when I began using the method in eliminating my distractions, even when it came to boys. Don't get me wrong; I've met some very great guys along the way, that remained to me as just friends, not only because I had a certain level of standards, but more importantly, I had to think about what was best for my vision. The truth of the matter is, I didn't need anything getting in the way of the vision I had for myself, and I don't mean to say that selfishly, but I do believe it is always important for you to do certain things for yourself personally, in terms of achieving the goals, dreams, and visions you have for yourself, in order to become the best version of yourself. I say that because the last thing you would want is for that person in your life getting in the way of chasing your dreams and seeing your vision come to past.

You have to understand that if you want to see the vision come to pass, you have to learn to accept the fact that not everyone in your life is going to have the capacity or ability in helping you see that vision come to pass. However, until you fully understand your purpose, vision, mission, dreams, and desires in life, only then are you able to recognize that the knowledge of yourself will determine the way you choose relationships, because if you know where you want to go in life, you already know from the start who can't get you there. In fact, for me personally, I had to do the same in understanding my purpose, vision, mission, desires, and dreams in life, so that I understand who can and cannot help me get there, because this method helps me regulate who I allow in my life on many different levels in terms of the things that are very important to me. In fact, in the end, I am going to want the right friends and the right man in my life that has the capacity to carry, push and add to the vision, in the same way, I would plan to do for them. I make that statement clear and precise because it is important to know whether the significant people in your life have the capacity, in terms of the level of thinking, courage, focus, and determination in helping you become the best version of yourself. That is part of being in any relationship that is built with teamwork, determination, commitment, trust, love, honesty, and encouragement. Although, I don't say any of this to make it seem like it is as easy to say than to live because, in reality, it is very hard, but I know for myself it will be worth it because the vision I have for myself is serious and something I'll never take lightly. In fact, it can often get a little harder here and there coming from someone who has been single for 19 years now, with a very small circle of friends.

However, it's a lot harder than you think, but it's not impossible, because as crazy as it seems, it was always about achieving and doing what was best for the vision in order to pursue something bigger than myself. However, I am not saying you should completely isolate yourself from people or not date, but you should pay close attention to the things in your life as far as relationships in understanding whether they're helping you become the best version of yourself, helping you achieve your vision or hurting you from seeing your vision come to pass. For I want the very best for you in achieving your vision, and that is why I wanted you to get the insider on ruling over the distractions in your life that want to do nothing but stop and hold back from God's very best for you. You deserve God's very best, so don't give up because you can do this.

Self-discipline

Once you are able to rule over the distractions, you've already taken a step into self-discipline. Self-discipline is so significant because it is essentially the key to achieving your vision. In fact, vision is the source of discipline because for a vision to be fulfilled, it requires a person to be trained and equipped along the way. However, what discipline does in terms of your vision is to make sure that you are doing the right things, that are beneficial to your vision, wasting no time. One of the greatest things self-discipline does that many overlook is the fact that it begins to reveal to you your true leadership. See, a true leader does not seek or chase after followers; instead, they attract followers through their sense of focus and self-discipline in regards to the dedication of their personal pursuit in life. The more disciplined you become, the more characteristics you have as a leader because people will begin to admire the way you discipline yourself in becoming the best version of yourself, that also helps them as well.

To give you a better understanding of self-discipline, think in terms of sports. As a previous athlete myself, I quickly learned the importance of self-discipline when it came to any kind of sport I played. The self-discipline came in terms of having to do certain things in order to put on my best performance, such as nutrition, weight lifting, studying, stretching, practice and rest. To perform your very best, you had to pay very close attention to so many things that had so much to do in determining how well you performed as an athlete. In the same way, we have to view our own lives in terms of achieving our vision by making sure that we are equipping and training ourselves for the desired outcome. When it comes to training and equipping yourself, that sometimes may look like doing certain things you may not always feel like doing, but in order for you to be ready to produce the vision, you have to put in the work. I love what Les Brown says, "to be successful, you must be willing to do the things today others won't do in order to have the things others won't have." You truly have to be willing to stay focused and disciplined even when those around you aren't because, in the end, you will understand that all the hard work and focus was worth it because you are walking in the fullness of your dreams and visions, because not for a minute did you give up.

I've learned for myself that in the process of pursuing the things beyond my reach, it was often challenging because it didn't always look the most coolest or fun thing to do compared my peers because only I understood what it is going take to see my visions come to pass. I had to learn how to be content in the places where God positioned me, that required me to come out of my comfort zone, do things I didn't think I was capable of, and simply help me stay focused on the goals, His plan, will, purpose, and vision for my life. In fact, once you begin to learn how to discipline yourself by training and equipping yourself with the right things, people will also begin to take notice in your self-discipline by admiring the way you live your life simply because it not only becomes something helpful to those around you, but it also causes people to want the product you have produced through self-discipline.

Think for a moment, in some of the most successful athletes we know of today, like Lebron James for instances, who had a rough start from the beginning but eventually worked his way up because he discovered the gift that was placed within him, which required him to work and develop the gift through a matter of being focused and discipline throughout the process. Lebron did everything he could do in becoming the best basketball player he was capable of being, resulting in there being so many people that looked up to him because of the product which he produced through focus and discipline. When he learned how to discipline himself in the certain areas of his life that were going to in the long run push his vision, in the end, it became something people admired, that eventually led to the product he produced through self-discipline, becoming something people were willing to pay to watch him do. In fact, when we learn to stop seeking success and start seeking to become a person of value, only then would we not only learn and discipline ourselves to become valuable, but people will take notice and be willing to invest in us, all because we learned to value ourselves.

Sometimes, we miss the opportunities self-discipline lays out right before us because we don't necessarily learn how to fully take our self-discipline as seriously as we should because, in the end, the success of our life counts on it. So, it is so important that you understand to take self-discipline seriously because if you don't, well, it then shows how unimportant your vision is to you. What we constantly miss is the fact that vision not only dictates everything in our life, but it also simplifies everything as well. It is why self-discipline is significant in terms of vision because once you have a vision; you begin to understand that everything you do is supposed to be motivated by your vision.

CHAPTER 5
THE GREAT OPPOSITION

"You face your greatest opposition when you're closest to your biggest miracle". -T.D Jakes

Some of the most well-known artist we know of today not only created some of history's most phenomenal pieces of artwork, but also faced times of great opposition during the process. Michelangelo, for instance, is well known for one of the most remarkable pieces made in art history, known as *The David*. However, what many don't know is the great opposition Michelangelo had to face in the process of creating this remarkable piece that eventually led to him doing one of the most impressive things throughout his entire career. The great opposition Michelangelo had to face was whether or not he was able to fulfill his vision even when it was said and believed to be impossible. However, Michelangelo was able to persevere even in the midst of one of the greatest oppositions he had to face only because, in the end, he refused to let anything thing stop him or get in the way of fulfilling his vision, even when it all seemed impossible.

Michelangelo was able to turn what was known as the "Giant", marble slab, into nearly a 17-foot-tall breathe taking beautiful sculpture known today as *The David*. This piece not only marked one of the greatest highlights in Michelangelo's career, but it marked a moment in conquering one of the greatest opposition that lied right in front of him, that eventually led to him becoming a more courageous and outstanding artist in the long run. It also caused him to be a success from that moment forward in all that he did, all because his vision always stood stronger and greater than any opposition that came his way. I tell you all of this to give you a better understanding, and an example of what facing great opposition looks like.

Opposition is described as something that causes resistance in action, the one thing that holds you back in completing the task. While opposition, of course, can seem like something unpleasant, if it is handled in the right manner, works out for you in the long run. It comes down to understanding how to face opposition in a way that doesn't cause you to give up or lose hope in your vision, but instead, becomes the stepping stones in achieving your vision that enables you to pursue something beyond you.

The Test

It all begins with a test, a test set up to determine whether or not the vision is real. You can get to this very point in your life, even with all of the previous fundamental steps I've shown you and still not have a real vision because your greatest opposition is going to test it. Any vision without opposition, in the end, is just an illusion. Once you fully understand that, only then you will you be able to determine what visions are real or just illusions that you might have fantasized about. However, it is important that you understand that the test is just a wake-up call, not something you should completely throw your entire life, dreams or desires away because of. As hard as it seems, it is, in fact, a requirement that you face opposition when it comes to your vision because, in the end, the results are remarkable. The test of opposition can come from the things we see, such as our sight, the things we hear, and the things we have previously been through in our life. When you have a vision that you are focused and disciplined on, don't think for a moment that you can stay comfortable where you are, thinking that there is nothing that can stop you, because, in reality, there will be.

Opposition works very differently than distractions because the thing with distractions is, the fact that you can walk away from them, while opposition is something you have to fight your way through, meeting face to face. For instance, one great opposition I had to face, dealt with my love and passion for art. I had been doing art since elementary up until now as a sophomore in college. However, I would often get asked why I didn't go to school for art, and it was primarily because it was something I believe I could continue to master and learn new techniques on my own through observation and helpful resources like I always did before. So, I continued doing art in my free time and that free time consisted being at home creating art. However, my parents were not a big fan of me doing any kind of art, even after I turned my room into a semi-art studio. At the time, I was in the process of remodeling my room, and I decided that I would not buy any artwork or canvas to hang in my room, instead, I would create them all myself. This, however, did not settle very well with my parents because they didn't even understand at all how it was all going to be done, in the period of time I had. Although, during the process of creating the pieces of artwork, I was eventually banned from doing any kind of artwork inside the house because of how messy the process was in creating the pieces of art. Being banned from the thing I love doing the most, made me feel like all the hard work and time I put into creating the pieces was all for nothing, and I began to feel like it was all over in creating the room I visioned for myself. However, there was something in me that couldn't just give up, so I had to find another way to get it done.

Throughout the process, it became a lot harder than I thought in making it happen because, good art requires a great matter of time, especially if you have different finishes and custom framing involved. However, when all 12 pieces of artwork were completely finished and hung all around throughout my entire room and bathroom, it honestly left my parents in complete shock because of everything I had visioned for my room came out way better than I expected. Although, it was only possible because I did not let opposition get in the way of fulfilling the vision I had for my room and nothing was going to stop me from making it happen. In fact, according to my dad, the big masterpiece I had made for my room is now the best piece of artwork we have throughout the entire house. I don't tell you all this for nothing; I tell you this to give you an example of how opposition can get in the way of even the simplest things you try to accomplish throughout your life. I also tell you this so that you understand it's something I've personally always had to deal with multiple times in my life in order to fully understand the reasoning behind it. In fact, the greatest thing throughout the entire process is how I was able to tap into the things in which I did not know I was capable of creating or doing that eventually led to one thing after another. It's the fact that if I had not gone through the opposition and let it get the best of me, a lot of the great things that I was able to produce through it would have never happened. For opposition has oddly in some ways become one of the things I look forward to regardless of how stressed and overwhelmed I get because, after going through different levels of opposition over time, you'll begin to stand firm in knowing that you can conquer and win the fight.

What you have to take into consideration is that regardless of the opposition you face, your vision must always be stronger because, in the end, the opposition will always be there to test your vision and test who you become throughout the process.

The Fight

As a result of opposition testing your vision, it will also reveal your fight. The term fight usually has to deal with aggressive measures that arise from things which you don't take lightly. To face your opposition, you must be willing to fight for your vision, the vision which you do not take very softly. However, I am talking about the kind of fight that you are willing to risk it all for in seeing your vision come to pass, even in the situations where seems to be going wrong, only then will the fight in you be revealed. It is the kind of fight that doesn't give up even when all hell breaks loose; you have to be able to stand firm and know that you can and will take it on. When it comes to your vision and protecting it, you have to learn how to push and fight through the opposition until you see your desired vision right before you. Sometimes, that means fighting the opinions of others who may try to tell you who you are or what you can and cannot do because, in the end, God is the determining factor of who you are and gives you the ability to do all things through Him. One of the best ways that will help you fight is knowing the divine source of all.

God goes before you in fighting the battles you were never meant to fight alone because, in the end, you cannot face the hard and impossible things alone, you need someone that will never forsake you even when everyone or everything is against you. Part of the fight requires more than your own ability; it requires divine power and authority that can overrule any kind of circumstance in your life that constantly tries to tear you down and destroy the thing God has placed in you. When you begin to learn and understand that you are never in this life alone because God is always with you and goes before you, you will begin to fight in a way where you have no choice but to win. You have the greatest of all right beside you to remind you that you are not in this alone and that you are more than a conquer.

The Win

In the end, it's a win because you began to learn how to fight for your vision with the mighty power of God by your side. Opposition is what God uses to shape and reveal to you, the real you which He has created. Only then, is He able to show you where your true strength lies, which is in Him, and you can see what great things you are capable of when you go through the great opposition. The greater the opposition we go through in our life, the closer we get to seeing our vision happen right before our lives. It is usually the last thing that holds us back from receiving all the great opportunities and things God has always had in store for us, but you see, God has to see whether or not He can trust us with the vision, which is why He uses opposition as a way to test our fight, desires and our character.

To give you a deeper understanding, I find it fascinating how Michelangelo's process in creating *The David*, resembles the actual biblical story of King David. The big marble slab was known as the "Giant" before it became *The David*. However, there is a story in the Bible; many are familiar with involving young David defeating the Philistine giant, Goliath. In this story, it focuses on a young man after

God's own heart who was courageous enough to do just about anything because He understood he was never alone and knew all things were possible with God. Before young David even came face to face with Goliath, he started as a just a young boy who herd the sheep, wrote poetry, played and sung songs. However, little did David know that everything he had been doing all of his life was all part of God's plan in equipping and training him to become a mighty warrior and King. That is why David volunteered to take down the Philistine giant because he saw an opportunity to not only honor God, but fight for the Israelites and the mighty God he served. But he had to face another great opposition that laid right before him in order to fulfill his vision, conquering Goliath.

However, this had not been the first time David faced opposition in his life because even when he was just a shepherd's boy, he had to face a lion and a bear that were among his sheep, when it is said that "the Lord that delivered me out of the paw of the lion, and out of the paw of the bear, He will deliver me out of the hand of this Philistine". (1 Samuel 17:37). David believed after everything he had been through, and how God was with him every step of the way, that without a doubt, it was all possible because God had never forsaken him or failed him, God was always the reason for David's victory. With just a slingshot and stone, young David was able to kill Goliath, making him a great hero to the Israelites. This is why *The*

David, is personally one of my favorite pieces of artwork in art's history because to me, it resembles not just the great biblical story of David, but how God used an ordinary man who faced a giant in front of him in which he conquered, in creating a piece of art that only would've been possible through the help of the mighty hand of God.

This ordinary man, Michelangelo would have not only created a breathtaking piece of work but, it would forever be a remarkable piece of work that symbolized one of the greatest stories in the Bible, of a man after God's own heart. However, more importantly, I believe *The David* does not only symbolizes the story of David, but resembles the story of all of us in the victory, failure, tragedy, and betrayal that happens throughout our lives, that leads us to understanding how a perfect God chooses to love imperfect people like us. God chooses imperfect people like us to love in helping us through every difficult and hard opposition in our lives because, He wants us to understand that as long as we depend on Him through His strength and power, we are to set up to conquer and defeat any and everything that seems impossible, through the mighty hand of God that covers and protects us from any weapon that tries to prosper.

"The true work of art is but a shadow of the divine perfection." –Michelangelo

Chapter 6
Hidden Potential

"Don't accept the opinions of others because they do not see what great and valuable potential is inside of you." -
Myles Munroe

When Michelangelo saw the big piece of marble slab right in front of him, he saw something full of great potential, *The David*. However, what many don't know is that while Michelangelo was trying to find a block of stone in which he could create a masterpiece for the Medics, eventually he found himself on the street of Florence, where a huge block of marble laid on wooden trestles filled with overgrown weeds, covered with dirt. I just want to point out that out of all the places he could've looked, he happened to find something that caught his eye after the many times he walked past this street where this piece of marble laid. It was only the very last time he stopped to look at the marble and begin studying it, only to reveal to himself that he saw something he visioned to be David, seeing it in its entirety.

This goes deeper than it seems because when you go back and understand the story of David, this might just blow your mind. Young David was not only a shepherd boy, but he was a young boy that his own father and older brothers overlooked and forgot, only seeing just a boy who herds the sheep and goats. However, when the time came to find the next King, David's father Jesse, presented to Samuel all of his sons who he believed were worthy enough to be the next King, except David. David's father didn't even think for a moment that David would be a possible candidate in becoming the next King because he was the youngest, smallest, and even the least likely to become King in his own father's eyes. David's father chose his other older brothers based on their age and appearance. However, while David's own father and older brothers saw no potential in him, God saw so much potential in him because he didn't look on the outside like men, he looked on the inside of David and saw his heart. In the same significant way, Michelangelo saw something great out of a large piece of the slab that was covered in filth and simply overlooked; he was then able to create one of the world's greatest sculptures ever made, all because he saw great potential in something that looked unworthy to be used. I personally believe that is the same way God often sees us, while others may overlook us and only sees what lay on the outside, God looks past everything that is on the outside of us and looks at this most important thing of all, our heart, which only then He is able to reveal to us our true potential.

Many of us haven't even experienced or recognized the true potential that lies inside of us because we become comfortable with just the things we have accomplished or done in our lives and believe that that is it. I hate to break it to you, but everything that you have done up until this point of your life doesn't even compare to the things you are truly capable of. When you begin to understand your true potential, it changes everything in the way you view yourself, the things you do, and simply the way you live your life.

Greatest Tragedy

I'll never forget coming across a reading that made such a profound statement that completely changed my view on potential. Dr. Myles Munroe explained a life-changing statement in how the wealthiest place on earth does not lie in the gold mines or the oil fields, but the wealthiest place on earth lies in cemeteries all around the world. The cemeteries acquire the most wealth in the entire world, because what lays in that very grave is dreams and visions never fulfilled, simply a graveyard full of potential. It's a tragedy to see people's dreams and visions die with them that not only would've created great wealth, but change the world. It is truly sad to see books that were never written, paintings that never were painted, businesses that were never created, songs that were never written, movies never created, and so much more all because it now lays all in the grave.

I personally believe that one of the greatest tragedies in life is to not only to live a life not knowing your purpose but more so, die full of the dreams and visions still in you, that you wished to do but never made it to the point in your life to fully understand your true potential to actually do them. The last thing I would personally not ever want for you is to never tap into the things in which God has placed inside of you, that little did you know would change the world you live in right now. However, I also believe one of the greatest tragedies in terms of our potential is not understanding where our true potential comes from. We often make a mistake in thinking that our potential comes from the previous things we've accomplished in our lifetime, to only then create a standard for yourself that says I have the ability to do things based on the previous things I have done. However, in reality, it was never meant to be that way because your potential is in fact, not based on the things in which you have already done, your potential is based on God.

Think of it this way, the visions and dreams that are placed in your mind that seem way beyond your reach or even something you honestly could never see yourself actually becoming, requires the ability which you do not have yet, only God does. In fact, those kinds of dreams and visions are things God places in you because only He understands that it is impossible for you to do it alone, but only through Him; He is able to reveal to you your hidden potential. However, what you must understand is God doesn't place anything in you if He doesn't already see the potential in you. Most of the time, those dreams and visions have more to do with revealing our true potential than we really think. Potential is all that you can do, but you have not done yet, which means that everything you have had the ability to do up until this point is actually no longer potential, it is something you have already done, while potential is everything that is still in you. In fact, some of the best advice that I've ever heard in terms of potential is that when you ever feel that you have done the best you could do, you actually just died. The moment I heard that, it blew my mind because it's so true!

You should never ever be impressed with the things you have done because only then will it stop you from doing things you could do. It's all about understanding that there is way more where this has come from, and so much more God has put inside you, that you have an entire lifetime to discover. One of the greatest things about potential is that it lies in every single human being, for God has placed hidden treasure in us all to constantly discover until there's nothing left. The last thing you want is to withhold the things which God has placed in you to make a great deposit here on earth for the next generation. What we sometimes completely overlook is the fact that while we don't live in the most perfect world, there is a perfect one who has created us and put something down on the inside of us to make the world we live in a better place not only for us, but for the generations to come, such as our children and grandchildren. The big question is whether or not you want to withhold the great wealth and brilliant ideas that lies right inside of you from the generations to come?

"You must decide if you are going to rob the world or bless it with the rich, valuable, potent, untapped resources locked away within you. -Myles Munroe

No Limit

One of the things that hold you back from experiencing your hidden potential is limits. Limits stop you from discovering your true potential because of the limits you've placed on yourself, believing that this is as far as you can go when in reality, you were meant to go beyond that. We often make a mistake in thinking there are certain limits in our life regarding how far we can go based on the current conditions in our life. However, what we sometimes don't even realize is our only limit is God. God is a limitless God, which means if He is the limit, there really are no limits in the things we dream or vision about doing or becoming. Once you understand that God is the limit, you start learning how to take the limits off in your life where you have the things you once dreamed of but somehow believed it never would be possible. Taking the limits off, takes the limits off in discovering your true potential. However, I personally believe the greatest limit that we must learn to take off in our life should start with taking the limits off of God. What we often misunderstand is that anytime we place limits on anything in our lives, we've already started placing limits on God and the things He plans to do in our lives. It is why placing limits off of God is important because only then are we able to take all the limits off in our lives. Little do we know that we often miss out on the great opportunities and blessings in our lives simply because we have placed limits in the areas where God initially plan to not only bless you beyond measures, but most importantly, help reveal to you your potential.

Since God is limitless, and God is the only limit, it only means that there is no limit to what you can do. The big thing you must grasp is the fact that when you began to take God out of the box of limits, it only opens you up to start dreaming, thinking, asking, and believing for things bigger than you have ever imagined for God to do in your life. It is the great start in discovering the great potential that lies within you once you learn to be opened and limitless to the things God wants to do for you and through you. Only then, will you be able to understand that because God is limitless and can do all things, you understand that there is nothing quite difficult for God to do in terms of the things you have dreamed and had visions about that seemed beyond you. I believe deep down in my heart that God wants to do miraculous things not only for you, but through you, that will completely change your life forever, in restoring the things in your life you once lost, the things you've dreamed of for the longest, and completely exceed your expectations, but He is waiting on you to take the limits off of Him. God can only do certain things in your life only to the extent to which you allow Him to do because God does not force anything on us, which is why He gives us a free will. No matter what condition you are currently in, I promise you that you lose nothing, but gain so much more when you begin to take the limits off of God in the things he wants to do for your family, finances, health, marriage, children, career, and so much more, but it is all up to you. I don't say this to bribe you into something that has false accusations; I tell you this because this is something I personally had to do in my own life, and once I decided to take the limits off of God, I am not lying when I say it changed my life.

Taking off the limits I previously place on God changed my life in helping me understand that since God is my only limit, there is truly nothing I can't do that He hasn't already given me the vision to do it, regardless of how unready and unqualified I may seem to feel. In the end, if God said it, I surely can do it because He sees the potential that I haven't fully discovered about myself. However, since I've learned to open myself up in the different ways God chooses to use me and do things through me, only then am I able to discover the potential in me, I would never have imagined I would find. This book, in fact, is a product of potential that has been hidden down on the inside of me that I honestly would have never actually imagined myself doing, especially coming from a college student who previously struggled writing just 2400 words essays. Although, the main point I am trying to get across is understanding that part of your hidden potential lies behind the limits you have placed in your life starting with God, and if you are truly ever going to start to pursue something bigger than you, it takes a bold step in simply making the decisions to take the limits off God, in which He plans to do exceedingly more than you might ever ask or think.

> *"Now to Him who is able to do infinitely more abundantly beyond all that we might ask or think, according to the power at work within us." -Ephesians 3:20*

Chapter 7
THE MISFIT

"You can't blend in when you're born to stand out". - Ryan Buchanan

One of the things I personally admire about art is the fact that the artist will do everything in their power to make their artwork stand out from the rest. Since all different types of art are created by different types of artist, each and every single piece of artwork is unique and different in its own way. However, what sells art is how different and unique a piece of artwork stands out from the rest. Artwork that seems to be unusual and unfamiliar to viewers seems to catch the most attention because of the fact it is a piece of artwork that standouts out, simply because it somehow doesn't seem to fit in with the rest. Art collectors would rather invest more into something that they have never seen before because they admire the work that has been done in making a piece of artwork standout among the rest. Although many artists will sometimes make printed copies of their artwork for canvases, etc. An art collector is not going to want a copy that can just be given and sold freely, allowing more than one person to have the same piece of artwork. An Art collector is going to want the authentic piece of artwork that was handmade by the artist themselves, which is only when they will be willing to pay a high amount for it, even if it is just art. What the art collector sees in the art that many other consumers do not see, is the indescribable value a piece of art holds in its detail, time and effort that is put in to bring a vision into illustration. Many see just a beautiful painting, drawing, etc., but it goes beyond that in understanding it is a real-life expression that gives viewers a piece of the artist's mind, feelings, emotions and more.

The greatest thing of all in the essence of art is truly in every single way, shape, and form of how unique and authentic it is because it is essentially a vision and dream birth into existence to create an illustration for viewers to capture. In fact, that no matter how hard artist even tries to consider copying another artist's piece of work, in the end, it's still going to be unique in its own way because it is not the same authentic vision that was birth inside the original artist, and since that vision came from the artist, it cannot rebirth the same exact authentic idea that was created and illustrated. That is part of what is happening now in this generation of all different types of artist around the world who strive to make their work stand out as much as possible, and the truth of the matter is, it is very hard. It's not as easy as it seems coming up with something authentic and original that hasn't been done before because it causes you to search deeper within yourself in order to produce something that this world has yet to discover or understand. However, it is also hard to develop something unique and authentic when everything around you influences you to be a replica of anything but yourself, causing you to settle for mediocrity. In fact, over the years, it has slowly become a norm to most of us because it is constantly what revolves around us and often clouds our perception in understanding what significance lies in being a misfit. It just happens to come to a point in our society where we've become more comfortable becoming anything but our authentic selves.

It's sad that we've begun to lose ourselves in other people, causing other people's identity, purpose, and lifestyles to become our own all because we rather fit into all the things of society regardless if they are good or bad, instead of being true to who we are and accepting the fact that we are different. In fact, just because you may be different, doesn't mean you have to change who you are just to fit in, because you have to understand that you were made this way for a reason in understanding the significance in being a misfit who doesn't settle for the mediocrity this world offers. I promise you, the last thing you want is to be afraid to stand out in a world that constantly pushes you to blend in.

"Mediocrity accepts the norm, pleases the crowd, and does what it can get by with. Maximum living pushes the norm, pleases God, and sets the standard for excellence."
-Myles Munroe

Ashamed

One of the most difficult things to deal with in terms of understanding that you were never made to fit in, is shame. You begin to feel ashamed of the fact that you don't fit in, all because those around you may judge you and treat you differently based on your authenticity. See, this here begins to create a big problem by letting other people's opinions and judgment rob you of your authenticity, all because you mistake it as something to be ashamed of. However, it not only robs you of your authenticity, but it also robs you in all of the different ways God is going to use you, starting with the things people may cause you to feel ashamed for. What we often make the mistake in understanding is the fact that if people begin to judge you and make you feel ashamed for something you had no complete control over, you should really be taking it as a compliment, not an insult. The reason I say that is because often, the enemy wants to rob you of your joy starting with who God created you to be, so since the enemy cannot physically destroy you, he will do anything in his power to cause you to destroy yourself, starting with accepting the validation and judgments of mankind. In fact, it is written that "there is only one lawgiver and judge, He who is able to save and to destroy. But who are you to judge your neighbor?" (James 4:12).

God is the only one that will be able to judge you because it is not in mankind's power to even give right judgment because it requires the supreme authority and power which is only given to God. However, one of the things we misunderstand is the fact that God can not only judge you because He holds the mighty power and authority, but simply because He is truly the only one who knows the real you since He is the one who created you. That is part of the reason we let judgment get in the way of so many things God has created us to do simply because we rather listen to the words of men who know absolutely nothing compared to a God who knows every single hair on our head, potential, purpose and the plans for our life, so why would we ever listen to the words of men over the words of God? Although, sad but the truth is, we would rather listen to the words of men in how we should live our life, what things we should do, what should we look like, who should we be with, and etc., when in reality God is supposed to give you the answers to everything regarding your life, because, in the end, He is the answer. He will be the one that helps you understand what significance lies in being proud of being a misfit. In fact, that is something I had to learn and discover for my own self in accepting the fact that I am a misfit and that is completely okay.

Growing up in my experience with school; I began to notice just how hard it was for me to fit in. While I had great friends throughout school, there were times I found myself trying to conform to things that were not of me just so I could somewhat fit in. I found myself gossiping about other people because that at the time was something everyone did, even though I knew it wasn't the right thing to do, I simply did so that I wouldn't seem like a complete outcast. However, as I began to get older and in high school, which was where I also began to have a deeper relationship with God, that started to change the way I lived my life. What I did not know is just how difficult it was now going to be to fit in because of the way I began to value my relationship with God, in doing what pleased Him simply because I began to understand the love God began to show me that began to change me in a way where I began to develop a great love and passion for people.

There were certain things I stopped doing such as gossiping about others because I had to learn to be true to myself, and that meant I could no longer conform to things that are not of me, simply because I grew up as a child always understanding the Golden Rule but never acted on it all because I would rather fit in than be true to what God created me to be. If there was any form of Scripture, I actually understood clearly during my childhood, that my parents advised always to use, it was the Golden Rule, "so in everything, do unto others what you would have do unto you". (Matthew 7:12). What I did not know was until I began to actually treat people the way I would want to be treated, only then did I really understand the significance behind it all. There were people who went through difficult things in their life and may not have everything like others, but because often, people don't know that, they judge them according to their outward appearance, causing them to get made fun of or talked about things they had no control over.

One of the things I stopped doing was talking down on people because, in the end, you truly have no idea what that person is truly going through. However, it did begin to put me in awkward situations at times because I had to watch the things I said, causing me to not always talk as much as I did. However, I'm not even going to lie when I say it wasn't easy because I was surrounded by people who only wanted to say very few positive things about certain people and more negative things. It caused me to become an outcast because I decided for myself not to talk down on people's name because that is the last thing I would want someone to do to me. As I continued to not conform to the things around me, it caused so many things in my life to change in a way I didn't necessarily expect. I watched some of my closest friends drift away, which was hard because I began to think something was wrong with me and that I did something wrong, but what I learned as I got older was the fact that not everyone accepts change and that is completely okay. Even as I got older, I still would find myself not fitting in even as a Christian. I often find myself not being able to fit in with other Christians because what many misunderstand about Christians is that not everyone is the same or has the same level of faith.

I've learned over the past few years of my life the importance of embracing the true me that often makes me stand out, because not only am I becoming the best authentic version of myself, but I am more than able to produce things that lie within me to stand out and be authentic. This is because whatever that is produce from you is just a reflection of you. It is the same way we are a reflection of God's image, we are able to embrace the power that lies in being a misfit and understanding in what ways God wants to use our own misfit selves in leading in an example for others to become the best authentic versions of themselves by staying true to themselves. I say all this to help you understand that just because you seem to not fit in anything, doesn't mean religion is going to change that for you, because, in the end, you were always created to embrace the thing that made you stand out. You should never be ashamed for something you were created to embrace because only then does it show your true authenticity.

Be Yourself

If there is anything that has helped me miraculously in accepting myself as a misfit, it was most defiantly learning how to just be myself. I went through a season of my life where I often struggled with understanding the real me because I would find myself trying to be anything other than the true me. I had often let people get in the way of expressing the real me because I cared so much about helping and being there for other people. I began to lose sight of who I was. I let people hinder the opportunities for me to truly express myself and just be the real me, all because I cared so much about people accepting me and not wanting people to judge me because of how different I was. However, I began to learn how to express myself as the real me and began to care less about what people thought of me. Although, it was not a very easy transition for me because I often felt alone and to myself. Part of the reason others didn't always accept me for who I really am was that they simply did not understand me at all or the way I lived my life. I've always been a very ambitious kind of person who went after anything I believed I could receive. My parents in fact, are witnesses because even when there were times they told me to take it easy or sometimes advice I shouldn't do this or that, they always knew no matter what they said to me, when it came to anything I felt strongly about doing, in the end, it was not going to stop me from going after it. However, along with being ambitious, I was the kind of person who was really into the deeper aspects of life and absolutely loved talking to different people about it. So, I would always try to learn more through the Word of God because I realized so many things about life that education didn't even come close to teaching me, only through God's Word was I able to be transformed in a way that made me think differently and have a completely different perspective on life. It was why I began to understand why people didn't always necessarily accept me for who I really was, because not everyone had the same interest as me and that is completely okay.

Although, I eventually had to find that balance in my life where I could be true to myself and not always as serious as people perceive me to be because I enjoyed having a great time with my friends where I was able to just constantly joke around with them. I learned just how finding that balance in my life changed everything in me and essentially becoming who God created me to be, to a point where I was able to express myself in so many different ways that related to so many people around me and that I was no longer in the bondage of people's perceptions, opinions, acceptance, or validations of me. I had to understand that, in the end, it didn't matter what people thought of me or whether or not they accepted me because, in the end, God is the one who has and will always accept me for who I am since He is the one that created me and that was all that truly mattered. I tell you all this because it is truly something I've had to deal with my entire life, but I had to make a decision to no longer care about what people say about me, the things that they think about me, or whether or not they accept me because God's opinion always and will forever overrule any opinion of mankind and that He didn't create me to fit in, because He made me purposely to standout. In fact, I began to develop the kind of mentality that could care less about what people think or say because they were not the ones who gave me my life in the beginning, God did, so there is truly no point in losing sleep or energy over the things people say.

It is so important to understand to be yourself because God made you special by making you one of a kind, so why would you ever want to be anyone else other than yourself? God made no mistake in creating the beautiful, fearfully and wonderfully made person that you are. Even when others judge you, make you seem inferior, cause you to feel ashamed of who God created you to be, or never fully accept you for who you really are and all that you have to offer, I want to let you know that you are not alone because God loves you because He created you, and because He is a perfect God, He never makes mistakes, even with creating you. He made a perfect human being in His own eyes, even when others see otherwise. You stay focus on the things God says about you to help you let go and express the real you because I promise you, it is truly something you will never regret once you learn to live a life based on God's thoughts of you compared to mankind's. Only then will you begin to see the great, beautiful picture in understanding what it's like to pursue something beyond you, once you understand that you are not hindered by the judgments, opinions, and acceptance of others. Be you, my friend and watch it change the entire course of your life. Plus, He made you great, so go and be great.

> *"If your going to succeed, you need to stand out on your own. People respond to truth and authenticity." -Angela Mondloch*

CHAPTER 8
WORTH IT

"The climb might be tough and challenging, but the view is worth it. There is a purpose for that pain; you just can't always see it right away." -Victoria Arlen

As of today, Leonardo da Vinci's *Salvator Mundi* is listed as the highest known price paid for a painting, which is 450 million. The painting is of what Jesus was perceived to look like during the Renaissance, known as the *Salvator Mundi*, which is actually Latin for "Savior of the World". What many may have not known about Leonardo da Vinci is his passion for understanding creation, using science and art as a way for him to help to figure out the discovery of creation. Leonardo was not only an artist; he actually pursued multiple things within his lifetime that would eventually lead him to discovering all of creation. In fact, Leonardo pursued studies of anatomy, engineering, architecture, optics, and many more disciplines, but what all these had in common was the ideal art of creation. All of the things Leonardo did was simply based on a pursuit in discovering all that could be known about creation. That is when the creation of *Salvator Mundi* was finally painted after all the years of vigorous work and studies in understanding creation which led him to understanding God in all of the patterns he studied that resulted in what he called, "the infinite works of nature". In that very moment, Leonardo had discovered something that would not only change his life forever, but the lives of so many people who admired him for his intelligence in all that he did that simply started with a passion, which only then became a vision, that helped reveal his purpose in his life.

You see, personally, I admire Leonardo not only for his beautiful art but most importantly, the way he had such a strong vision, passion, and purpose that made all the hard and long work he did throughout his entire life be worth everything in the pursuit he had to discover creation. I have no doubt in my mind Leonardo understood what it was like to pursue something way beyond him because he let nothing stop him in the process of his discovery, even when many misunderstood him due to all the diverse pursuits in his life that eventually lead to the one thing that would begin to change everything. What I personally believe about Leonardo is that his pursuit had so much to do with not only discovering God's creation but understanding the depths of God. I personally believe that during the process, Leonardo caught a glimpse of something in God that completely changed the next course of his life from that moment. In all the years of his discovery, he understood that while he was pursuing something beyond him, there had always been something pursuing him, leading him to become what he will go down in history for. Leonardo da Vinci does not only go down in history for being one of the greatest artists ever known, but he goes down in history for something many people don't particularly know him for. Leonardo was a genius, who through his vigorous studies and work over the years, provided proof through his own artwork, the existence in the omnipotence of God through nature, starting with some of the simplest details such as color, light, the human body, and most importantly, creativity.

Through Leonardo's artwork, he was able to provide significant artwork that would lay down the foundation for artists after him, understanding where art solely came from, God. In fact, it was something the art during the renaissance was solely based on. I say all this to show you a great example of someone who understood the Art of Pursuit, not because he just happens to be an artist, but the fact that he knew how important and serious this pursuit was to him, even if it took his entire life to finally see it. You see, I believe deep down in my heart that Leonardo was chosen by God because God began to see just how Leonardo did everything in his power to find God and understand the things of God. However, I believe that Leonardo had no idea that he would end up going down in history as the most influential artist of the Reissuance and that the visions and dreams God placed within him would manifest into something greater than he had ever imagined, causing him to leave such a great legacy and value behind that is constantly admired and recognized today. I believe that God saw something in this man that He could use to change the world starting with the gift He placed inside of him.

You see, what I never mentioned was the initial purpose of my own pursuit because if I told you at the very beginning, it would just be a complete spoiler and you wouldn't be able to put all of the pieces together, in order to initially see the bigger picture. What made this pursuit so significant in my life is the fact that what I made the decision to pursue that was bigger than me, was God. You may have thought I was talking about a career or some sort, but essentially, my visions, dreams, desires, career, calling and purpose revolves and has everything to do with pursuing God. It is a level of understanding that means everything that I do in my life has everything to do with pursuing God, because I've begun to learn that when I start pursuing God, everything else follows such as my dreams, visions, careers, callings, and initially my purpose in life is revealed. Most importantly in my pursuit for God, I learned things that no one will ever be able to teach me except for God, in understanding that this pursuit is way more than just pursuing God, in fact, it is truly understanding the beauty and majesty of God that I personally view as art, in the way He uses everything that has ever happened to me for a greater purpose.

It is the type of art I see that is essentially produced from God in using me as His blank canvas, in creating the plans, dreams, visions, desires, and passions within me to resemble, in the end, the finished product. However, more importantly it is about understanding the beauty and majesty behind the pain, suffering, trials and tribulations that happen within our life, that God is able to use in such a way that eyes have not seen the great work that God is able to create within us that not only becomes the solutions to the problems in the world we live in, but also become a piece of work shown to the world that is able to resemble what great things God can do with the ugly, hopeless, defeated, forsaken, and broken pieces of His creation, by transforming them into the great beautiful work of art that has yet to be seen.

Patience

One of the things that are often overlooked in terms of trying to pursue anything is patience. Some of the greatest things in life require time, which means you have to understand just how important patience is. Patience, however, isn't something easy to learn or develop, because most of the time we want things right away. Any kind of dream or vision that you wish to see come pass, requires you to have a certain level of patience that doesn't make you lose hope in the one thing you are working so hard to see happen in your life. Although, one of the things that are often said about my generation, in particular, is just how often we want things fast and easy. As I've been around a lot of older people, I notice how if there is anything that is commonly said about my generation, it is that we often want things fast but don't necessarily want to put in the required work to get it, because of how long it takes. However, in reality, it is about things taking time, for the right things to unfold at the right time. The thing is, some of the greatest things not only take time to receive but it, in fact, is something worth waiting for. I say this only because it is honestly something that I've personally always struggled with, but when I began to become more patient in the things I personally wanted in my life, I began to learn the significance in patience and the great benefits that come with waiting. What people often misunderstand about patience is the fact that the lack of patience will often stop you from getting the whole.

You may find yourself at times, becoming impatient with certain things you want to see happen immediately in your life, so you often take it upon yourself to do just the thing you were previously waiting for. However, the problem is you miss out on the significance of patience because you've chosen to settle for what you can get, rather than receiving the better thing that comes only when you wait. For instance, it's like going shopping, and you decide that you what to go ahead and get the item you've been waiting forever to go on sale, however, two days later that same item goes on sale for 80% off and now you wish you would have just been patient and waited. What you have to understand is that there is an initial purpose behind any kind of wait in your life, revealing your true motives, character, and most importantly, building your patience. Waiting for current things to happen in my life has never been easy, in fact, I believe it is one of the hardest things for me because I do find myself at times wanting to compromise just so that I can receive certain things in my possession, but one thing that has helped me greatly is understanding that the longer I wait for certain things to happen as they should, the better the outcome is. The outcome is often greater than you expect, once you learn to wait on certain things in your life to happen because God never holds you back from receiving His very best, but what He is doing while you wait, is simply teaching and preparing you for the great things He has in store for you. What I often see waiting as is a time of preparing for the great doors God will open when I am ready to receive His very best.

The whole point in waiting isn't something that just seems like a waste of time, it is actually a time for development and preparation to take place, specifically for the promotions, relationships, finances, businesses, and all the great blessings God has for you, but without patience, none of this is possible. Think about it, some of the greatest opportunities we often miss out on are just a result of the lack of patience, causing us to settle for things that were never meant for us from the very beginning. It is easy to get impatient at times, but you have to constantly remind yourself that God has way more in store. When you learn to increase your level of patience for things in your life, things begin to happen on their own without you having to force anything because that is the way God created it to be. God is the only one that can open and close the doors in our lives regarding any kind of jobs, careers, promotions, relationships, etc., but as long as you try to continue doing things on your own, with your own ability, you will never fully receive God's very best, all because you couldn't wait for God to give it to you himself.

I often believe one of the most common things we often struggle waiting on, is the right relationships because, I truly believe in my heart that there wouldn't be as much brokenness as there is in relationships, if people didn't abuse patience and their time of waiting. I say that because I personally believe that one of the most significant moments of your life results in you being single and waiting on the right person. However, it is what you do in that waiting time that will often make or break the relationship. You see, while you wait on the right person, it is a time for personal development and preparation to also take place because, without this, I believe it causes problems. That is the time to develop the best version of yourself in understanding your true identity, purpose, passion, self-love, confidence, potential, goals, self-value, and most importantly, becoming whole. This is so important because I've seen so many people throughout my life suffer in relationships that they weren't fully ready to be in all because they didn't truly understand who they were, their value and self-worth, self-esteem, confidence, self-love, or wholeness, so eventually, the other person in the relationship abused the one thing they had very little preparation or development on. However, I am not a relationship expert or anything because I had not been in a real relationship myself, but I often, always observed my peers relationships and studied things regarding relationships so that I could learn from others and their experiences, as well as learn the from studies to try to help others and myself.

I say all this because we often let the people in our relationships define who we are, all because we've missed the significant steps of self-development and preparation, that helps us identify who we really are, allowing no one to treat us just any kind of way because we understand our value and we've learned to love ourselves even when others don't. If there is anything you should truly understand about your initial waiting time for a relationship, it is understanding the importance of being effective in the things you want out of your life and most importantly, becoming the best version of yourself, because there are certain things in your life that requires your full attention, determination, commitment, and time, that doesn't necessarily always have to be people, but your greatest dreams, visions, and desires beyond you. Eventually, you will know at the right time when you believe you are ready for a relationship when things are moving in the right direction, and you believe that that person would make a great addition to you and your life. Notice that I said addition because you are your own kind of person and anyone that is in a relationship with you, only adds to you because you are still the amazing person that you are with or without them, and you should never forget that.

"The time you are most prepared for dating is when you don't need anyone to complete you, fulfill you, or instill in you a sense of worth or purpose." -Myles Munroe

I went into great detail about relationships in particular because I've noticed that it is something we naturally struggle with in terms of patience, because we often misuse relationships in thinking that certain people will make our life complete, when in reality, it was never meant that way because you will never find true satisfaction in people, because we are not perfect and we make mistakes. True satisfaction only comes from God because He never runs out of love for you, He never stops pursuing you, and He is the only one that has the power to give you what no one on earth can give you, which is everlasting life. Although, if you keep searching for satisfaction in people, you'll never be complete or fully happy because only God can do that. In fact, what has often become rare in today's society is the significance of wholeness and how it has everything to do with any relationship you are in.

Wholeness is so important in terms of any relationship because only through wholeness, you understand that you are complete even without a significant person in your life, because you don't need to rely on different people to make you happy, complete, provide for you, or solve your problems and brokenness because the truth of the matter is, only God can do that. When we learn to become whole with God in terms of letting Him be the divine source for our needs, brokenness, happiness, and joy, we begin to view relationships differently and set ourselves up for the better relationships that add to everything God created us to be. I personally believe from the amazing relationships and marriages I've seen, that God will always lead you in the right direction of finding the right person in your life that resembles and magnifies God's, great love. That this significant person becomes the great resource from God that does not complete you, but adds to you in such a way that helps you benefit from each other, in being a great help in becoming and doing all the great things God has placed within each person, that becomes their initial purpose in pushing the greatness out of them for the better. However, while this is how I personally see great relationships, it might not be for everyone but what more importantly eventually happens when you give up on having patience is, you often settle for what is easy to get in your possession, all because you refuse to wait on the right man to pursue you or give up on pursuing the right woman.

However, whatever is easy in life to get is usually the easiest thing to lose, just to let that sink. I tell you all of this because this is everything I've had to personally learn for myself and what I learned, in the end, is just how great it has helped me in ways like no other, by simply increasing my level of patience. God, of course, has made it all possible because even in the times I wanted to give up on waiting, He constantly renewed my strength in ways that help push me to wait longer for certain things because I've learned to trust Him in the process, and as a result, I've received promotions, increase in my finances, life-changing opportunities and so much, more only because I decided that I would wait for God's very best and I will say it was definitely worth waiting for. I believe the same can happen for you when you begin to wait on the great things God has in store for you, because He wants nothing more than to give you His very best because He is deeply in love with you and understands that you deserve His very best, but He wants to see if you are willing to trust Him to wait. God wants to do a new thing in your life starting with building your patience in ways that help you become the best version of yourself and restoring you beyond your exceptions. I am not lying when I say the greatest things are worth waiting on because you don't really realize it until you've actually waited on something in your life that may have taken years to receive, but you appreciate it more than ever because you understand the wait was worth it all. Although, that, in fact, is the art in patience, seeing what you learn and who you become during the process that reveals something very beautiful and totally worth the wait when God is able to bless you with more than you asked for.

"When you learn to let go and learn to trust God, it releases joy in your life. And when you trust God, you're able to be more patient. Patience is not just about waiting for something, it's about how you wait, or your attitude while waiting." -Joyce Meyer

The same thing goes for just about anything you want to pursue that's bigger than you; it takes a life full of patience to see it come to pass in the end. Even in this pursuit for God and all the things He has promised me, patience is one of the greatest factors because along the way, I am constantly learning things each and every day in all of the things I am pursuing that pertains to my calling and purpose in life. However, I had to understand that it is going to take time for it all to fully manifest and that is something I just have to continue to trust God with and know that if He said I could do it, I can and will do it even if I am not nearly close to it.

The greatest reason of all in why I chose to pursue God above anything else is simply because I love Him with my whole heart, mind, and soul. He is the only reason I chose to live this way because I find great unspeakable pleasure in Him, that I will never be able to find here on earth. As I continue to pursue Him each and every day of my life, only then, He is able to lead me to the things that I am called and created to do here. However, pursuing God has never been easy because it is tough and challenging in all the ways I've explained in having to face feeling lost, brokenness, rejection, pain, trials, test, isolation, opposition, fear, judgement, tears, sacrifice, and much more, but while all this seems devasting, only God was able to make ways out of absolutely nothing. That indeed is the true beauty of it all and why this pursuit means absolutely everything to me because after everything that I have been through in my life up until now, I look back at my life and see how God used every good and bad aspect of my life growing up as a way to help me see beyond it all, to truly understand the great majesty that lies behind it all, being formed into His great masterpiece.

> *"If God is all I have, I have everything that I need." -John 14:8*

Chapter 9
Masterpiece Donation

"The value of life is not in its duration, but in its donation. You are not important because of how long you live, you are important because of how effective you live. -Myles Munroe

As an artist growing up, one of the hardest things I found very difficult for me to do was giving away my artwork. I constantly wanted to hang on tight to the pieces of artwork I worked very hard for and refused to give them away. When I was younger, I would sometimes wonder why people would even consider asking me if they could have a piece of artwork that I was finished with for a class. I didn't even understand that certain people had a great appreciation for art and even often made them feel a type of way. However, I was very greedy with my artwork, which did me no good since I eventually had to get rid of them anyway, but all because I was just thinking about myself in that moment, I missed my opportunity to give my art away to the person who actually admired it and wanted to keep it. Even as of today, I think differently about that situation in how that person might have seen something in my artwork that might have helped them or given them hope. There are often times in our lives where we miss out on the great opportunities in making the lives of the people around us better, simply because we've seemed to only care about the things regarding our own life.

There are some things we withhold from the people that God purposely created to use as a great resource in making the lives of the people around you brighter and better. You see, God did not create mankind to live alone or do things on their own; He initially created them as great compatible teams that had dominion over the earth and helped build the generations to come after them. However, things have become different over the years as God's creation began to drift away from compatibility in ways that made mankind divide from one another resulting in racial segregation, divorces, immigration, parties, religion, etc. What all these things have in common is separation that results in competitiveness and conflict. That is why unity is everything because while there are multiplicities of things, they all come as one for a greater good and outcome. I believe it is something we need more of today, because no matter who you are, what you do, or what you have been through, sometimes the only physical help you can get is initially through people. That is the way God, in fact, operates and does His great works, which is often through people so that He can reveal himself. However, the greatest part of it all is that God doesn't use the people that seem to have their lives completely together, he uses the people that others see and believe to be unqualified, qualified for the things He wishes to do. Although, while it may seem like a list of religious things you must do for God to use you, it, in fact, is not true.

One of the things I believe that is often misunderstood about God is thinking God has everything to do with religion when in reality; He is a God of relationship. We often believe in terms of religion that God asks us to do certain things like read our Bible, pray, fast, repent, love and be obedient so that we one day can go to Heaven. However, that is the perspective of a religious mindset thinking you have to work your way to Heaven. You see, what many overlook is the fact that God is a God of 'Kingdomship', where all He asks is to be in a relationship with you, and because you are in a relationship with God, you start falling in love with Him. When you begin to fall deeply in love with God, you begin to love the things He loves; you begin to do things that please Him because you love Him that much. You simply do things out of complete love, not religion. You may read His Word because you are in love with Him, so you constantly want to learn more and more about Him. You pray because you love hearing and speaking to God, being able to call unto Him. You may fast so that you can clear out the things in your life that seem to be getting in the way of hearing from God clearly, or you may be in desperate need of His great love and presence, so you make special arrangements to ensure there is great intimacy. You repent because you understand that your relationship is built on honesty, transparency, trust, and forgiveness. You are obedient because you understand that your relationship with God is also built upon submission and trust that whatever He says to do, must and will be done because you love Him to that extent in your life. You simply love Him because He shows you the type of unconditional love the world can never offer you that cause you to love in a way that is radiant in everything you do.

I break this all down into detail to show you the personal details of my own relationship with God in how it is solely a relationship based on love, not works. That there are levels to the relationship in terms of getting to a point where your love for God is so deeply strong that you begin to do everything in your power to become part in building His Kingdom, that the lives around you would be introduced and given a better opportunity and a greater start of life, by walking in the fullness that God desires for His creation. In fact, only through this great 'kingdomship' that is built on a great foundation of love, lies the power to bring Heaven down on earth. It is why God's relationship with us is exclusively based on love and not works because love has great power in changing lives forever. However, while there are people who desire to change the world, it should be noted that the only way you are truly going to change the world is simply through love.

We think changing the world has to do with actions, but in reality, all it takes is simply walking in love because it is the one thing that is going to make a greater impact on the lives of people. The problems we often deal with in our society today only rise from the lack of love, because we often see the opposite of love, which is hatred in people, ourselves, the things we do, etc. There is a lack of love because people who don't know what love is, don't know how to walk in love. However, it must also be noted that love is God and God is love, so it is only proof that those who don't know what love is, rises from not knowing who God is since He is love. In fact, since there are people who don't know what God's love feels like, they often misunderstand what love looks like. Part of loving God results into being able to love yourself, and the more you begin to learn about God in what He is and the way He created you, you will begin to fall in love with who He created you to be. You will begin to understand the significance in self-love and just how it has everything is showing what real love is to those around you.

You see, the truth is, you will only be able to love someone else the extent to which you love yourself. It's about understanding if you can learn to love yourself, you will begin to learn how to truly love people in the way you see yourself, by embracing and encouraging the great things about them. However, there is a lack of love because we have people who are filled with the love of God, but often withhold it from people through arrogance, judgments, bitterness, unforgiveness, jealousy, etc., and end up robbing people from the love of God. It's sad but true because these are often people who know God, such as Christians who sometimes refuse to show love to those who have hurt them deeply, all because they begin to believe they're too "holy" and "saved", or simply become jealous and bitter based on the things God has blessed others with. It is not about judging people for the things that they have done or the way people chose to act, believe or choose to live their life, it is more importantly about embracing the great person that they are, regardless of the things they do or have done through love, by seeing everyone the way God sees His creation, as a great masterpiece. The truth of the matter is, God's love is so deeply great and life-changing that the last thing that needs to happen is people withholding His great love that was initially created to be shared. If we ever want to see any kind of positive change throughout our world, we must understand the greater significance and power of love and how it can changes the lives around us for the better, but we must learn to walk in love ourselves to see our world change for the greater good.

"Above all, love one another deeply, because love covers a multitude of sins." -1 Peter 4:8

Gift

"The meaning of your life is to find your gift. The purpose of your life is to give it away." -Pablo Picasso

Part of changing the lives around us starts with the gift God has placed down on the inside of us. Believe it or not, everyone has a gift in them that God created specifically for them to dominate. However, we often misuse our own gifts in thinking we have none, causing us to copy other people's gifts, that they were originally gifted with. What many misunderstand about God and the gifts He places within us is the fact that God will only grace you for the things in which He created you to do, especially in terms of any of the gifts He has placed in you. However, we often think we have no significant gifts to offer to this world because of the things we been through or the way we have been raised, causing us to believe that there is no possible way God can place something significant in someone like us. I hate to break it to you, but that is entirely not true because it doesn't matter who you are, what you have been through, or what you have done in your past, God still chose you regardless of it all, because He loves you. It truly comes down to discovering the gift He has placed in you because it takes time to not only discover them but also develop. However, it is also important to understand that gifts come in all different shapes and sizes because while it seems like others have these phenomenal gifts, it starts to make you think that the gift that you have is inferior compared to others and can't do any good compared to other people's gifts. The truth is you will never really know what your gift is capable of doing if you never exercise it and develop it unto its fullness.

Everyone has a gift, but we sometimes think other people's gifts are better than our very own just because they were able to develop it into its fullness. Every gift starts as something small, but it's what you do with the gift that determines its outcome, in whether or not you work at it in order for it to develop into its fullness. You never want to mistake your gift as something inferior or insignificant compared to others, because the truth is, it takes time, practice and patience for the gift to be fully manifested in the way God created it to be. That is often why people end up having to put in the extra work and skill in manifesting the gift that is in them. The biggest thing you must understand is that a gift loses its significance and meaning without the act of giving. God did not place such wonderful and life-changing gifts within you, just to manifest for yourself. God placed those great gifts in you for the benefit of others, so that you would be able to share and give to the world the life-changing gifts in which God has placed specifically in you. Your gift doesn't always have to be as extravagant as you think; the gift that is placed within you could be something as simple as the gift in caring for others. It truly doesn't matter how insignificant you may view your gift because, in the end, when you learn how to exercise it in the right manner, it becomes something greater than you imagined in making a great impact, helping or changing the life of someone, who needed your gift.

The most important thing of all in terms of your gift is understanding how to be a good steward of it. Being a good steward of your gift requires you follow through in all the fundamental steps and methods that is previously talked about because without an identification, purpose, pain, brokenness, a vision, dream, boldness, faith, focus, discipline, courage, opposition, and most importantly of all, God, your gift can easily be abandoned by the things and people of this world if you let them get in the way of fully manifesting the gift. I tell you all this because you will never be able to experience the fullness and joy that comes with sharing and giving away the magnificent gift God has placed in you. You begin to get a full revelation in your existence of why God created you the way you are, the things you have had to go through, and why it was worth it all in the end. When we begin to understand this fully, we begin to understand that we don't exist for our own being, we exist in helping the people we love and the people we are constantly surrounded by each and every day of our lives because we weren't made to live life alone, but constantly be a great help in getting through this thing we call life.

God initially put something on the inside of you because He didn't create you to just exist, even in the environments, places, and things you have been in and through, it was all part of God's plan in manifesting the thing that is on the inside of you, in order for it to be placed on earth. In fact, God placed something so special in you that He refuses to give up on the thing He has placed down on the inside of you, even when you decide you want to start giving up. That indeed, is the great beauty in the gift that is received from God, that He is able to not only make ways for you, but transform you, give you great joy in existing, and completely change the world around you.

> *"Your existence is evidence that this generation needs something that your life contains." -Myles Munroe*

Gift to You

In the same way, God placed a great gift in you; He has done the same for me. This, in fact, is my personal gift to you in understanding the Art of Pursuit that not only has the ability to completely change your perspective in life, but help you in multiple areas of your life in accomplishing and doing things you would have never imagined you would ever be doing. I share the Art of Pursuit with you because it is something that is so close to my heart and something I cherish and live by, that has benefited me in ways like never before, and that is truly what I hope for you. I hope you get a better understanding of how pursuing God can completely change everything in your life, being able to conquer and face anything that life throws your way because you have the mighty power of God at work within you to defeat and accomplish all things through Him. The art of pursuit gives you the understanding that when you begin to pursue God, there is truly nothing impossible for you to pursue, conquer or achieve in this life because you have the greatest source of all in helping you become the very best version of yourself each and every day. The Art of Pursuit is not some religious rituals you must follow in order to get to Heaven, if anything, it is Kingdom fundamental tools in helping you not only become the best version in which God created you to be, but simply having the power and ability through God to bring Heaven down on earth. Also, being able to make the lives on earth and earth itself a better place through the Kingdom fundamental tools that are able to give people all around the world the great opportunity in living beyond their limits, conditions, situations, and more.

It's truly about understanding the great impact that is created in the process of the pursuit for God, that releases the beauty and majesty along the earth, allowing people to receive more than what life has to offer through God, who is able to create and build masterpieces around the world, that leaves a great legacy for the great generations to come. This pursuit is art to me in how God starts with a blank canvas and is only then able to create something throughout the process into something quite breath-taking that can change lives, bring revival, and completely create something that is completely priceless and precious in His eyes, He never stops loving or pursuing. The Art of Pursuit is the art in pursuing something that has always pursued you in all the days of your life in order to eventually reveal to you the greatness and power that lies within you to do things that only God has the ability to do through you. I pray and hope that this becomes a great resource in pursuing all the great things God calls you to, letting nothing stop you in the process, but staying confident and standing still in who God is and all that He can do. You, my friend, are not alone in this pursuit for a greater life, because God loves you like nothing you will ever experience through this world, and He is truly waiting for you to pursue Him so that He can restore and bless you beyond measures. I made this decision myself, and I know for a fact that I'll never regret making the decision in pursuing God with my life because there are just so many majestic and phenomenal things that I have experienced that I'll never have the words to explain because I wouldn't be where I am or who I am today, if I had not made this decision. I hope you even consider in letting God change your life and the lives around you in becoming, doing, and pursuing the things way bigger than you, in which He purposely created you to do.

> *"But seek first The Kingdom of God and His righteousness and all these things shall be added unto you." Matthew 6:33*

ABOUT THE AUTHOR

19 year old Corlissia Moore was raised in Burleson, TX and shares a great passion for art which she loves creating during her free time as well as reading and helping people in every way she has the ability to do so. She was a raised in a great household under wonderful parents with two brothers. Growing up in a Christian household, her parents raised her and her brothers in the teachings of God, and these teachings helped shape Corlissia in ways she'll never be able to fully describe in words and eventually led to her falling in love with a great, mighty, powerful God that never stopped showing her just how loved she was each and every day of her life. As she began to grow deeper in her relationship with God, things became more and more challenging as she continued her walk with God. What she learned as she continued to walk into the things that God has called her to is that it will always look challenging and will often times feel uncomfortable but in the end, that is what it looks like to pursue something bigger than you. In the end, it is worth absolutely everything because nothing will ever compare to the great abundance that is placed over your life when you walk into the fullness of who God has called and created you to be.

www.ingramcontent.com/pod-product-compliance
Lightning Source LLC
LaVergne TN
LVHW041230080426
835508LV00011B/1132